A Moral Universe Torn Apart

A Moral Universe Torn Apart

Ben Shapiro

Creators Publishing
Hermosa Beach, CA

A Moral Universe Torn Apart
Copyright © 2018 Creators Publishing

Cover art by Peter Kaminski

CREATORS PUBLISHING
737 3rd St
Hermosa Beach, CA 90254
310-337-7003

ISBN (print): 978-1-945630-94-1
ISBN (ebook): 978-1-945630-02-6, 978-1-942448-46-4

First Edition
Printed in the United States of America
1 3 5 7 9 10 8 6 4 2

A Note From the Publisher

Since 1987, Creators has syndicated many of your favorite columns to newspapers. In this digital age, we are bringing collections of those columns to your fingertips. This will allow you to read and reread your favorite columnists, with your own personal digital archive of their work.

—Creators Publishing

Contents

What to Expect in 2014

January 1, 2014

2013 was a year of revelations, a year of possible turning points. For nearly two decades, since Ronald Reagan left office, America moved steadily in the direction of the left, both culturally and politically. When the Soviet Union fell, optimistic scholars believed the world had shifted inexorably in the direction of free markets and liberal democracy. Instead, the West gradually embraced bigger government and weaker social bonds, creating a fragmented society in which the only thing we all belong to, as President Barack Obama puts it, is the state.

All battles for the soul begin with culture. And while the battle against Obama's unprecedented growth of government started with the tea party victories of 2010, the cultural battle against the left didn't truly take until 2013. The seeds were planted for this cultural battle in earnest in 2012, when Obama and his Democratic Party allies put race, sexual orientation and abortion at the core of his reelection campaign. Americans were told by the media that Obama's competence mattered less than the fact that half the country was mean, nasty, racist and homophobic. Todd Akin's absurd comments on conception via rape were the issue, Americans were told, not the imminent takeover of the health care system; Obama's sudden support for same-sex marriage was the issue, not his devastating regulatory state; George Zimmerman and Trayvon Martin were the issue, not the destruction of entire swaths of the United States via leftist governance.

And it worked. Conservative Americans, bludgeoned into silence on cultural battles, decided to focus entirely on Obama's economic buffoonery. Unsurprisingly, it didn't work; culture, as my friend Andrew Breitbart was fond of stating, is upstream of politics.

2013 marked a turning point. From Chick-fil-A to "Duck Dynasty," conservative religious Americans found their footing: Whether you are for or against same-sex marriage, it is plainly un-American to override someone's religious beliefs in the name of your politics. Conservative Americans seemed to realize, for the first time in a long time, that the battle over same-sex marriage came wrapped in a larger battle over religious freedom. And they fought back, and won.

Meanwhile, conservatives began to fight back against the left's uncorroborated assertion of right-wing racism. While MSNBC focused laser-like on one Confederate flag at an anti-Obamacare rally, those same MSNBC hosts laughed at Mitt Romney's adopted black grandchild (Melissa Harris-Perry), suggested that someone ought to "p***" and "s***" in Sarah Palin's mouth (Martin Bashir), used anti-gay slurs (Alec Baldwin), shook down businesses over race (Al Sharpton) and labeled words like "black hole" and "Chicago" racist (Chris Matthews). Race, the right realized, was an obsession only for the left.

And in the aftermath of the left's successful 2012 "war on women" meme, the right began to fight back, too. Beginning with the left's attempted deification of amoral Texas state Sen. Wendy Davis, who filibustered for 11 hours on behalf of the murder of 21-week-old fetuses, the right refused to be cowed. Abortion is a real moral issue with real lives at stake, and no amount of leftist badgering could back conservative Americans off their attempts to protect the unborn.

The cultural battles gradually made their way into the political arena, too. Freed from the burden of the beige and blundering Romney campaign, conservatives stood up against the growth of government on moral, not merely practical, grounds. Obama's signature program began to collapse the moment Americans awakened to the deep immorality of government-controlled medical care. Sen. Ted Cruz's government shutdown strategy, right or wrong, highlighted conservative opposition to the state as cradle-tograve caretaker. American distrust of government, for the right reasons, soared.

This does not mean the battles are over for conservatives. They're just beginning. The media have already geared up toward nominating Hillary Clinton in 2016 (The New York Times whitewash of Benghazi this week was only the beginning). The DC-run Republican Party has a disheartening way of crippling its own conservative base in order to cut deals. But 2013 could go down as the year that conservatives moved beyond standing athwart history shouting "stop," and began shoving in the opposite direction, which could make 2014 historic.

Why Socialism Is on the Rise

January 8, 2014

It took capitalism half a century to come back from the Great Depression. It's taken socialism half that time to come back from the collapse of the Soviet Union. In New York City, avowed socialist Mayor Bill de Blasio has declared that his goal is to take "dead aim at the Tale of Two Cities" -- the gap between rich and poor. In Seattle, newly elected socialist city Councilmember Kshama Sawant addressed supporters, explaining, "I wear the badge of socialist with honor." To great acclaim from the left, columnist Jesse Myerson of Rolling Stone put out a column telling millennials that they ought to fight for government-guaranteed employment, a universal basic income, collectivization of private property, nationalization of private assets and public banks.

The newly flowering buds of Marxism no longer reside on the fringes. Not when the president of the United States has declared fighting income inequality his chief task as commander in chief. Not when Senate Majority Leader Harry Reid, D-Nev., has said that America faces "no greater challenge" than income disparity. Not when MSNBC, The New York Times and the amalgamated pro-Obama media outlets have all declared their mission for 2014 a campaign against rich people.

Less than 20 years ago, former President Bill Clinton, facing reelection, declared "the era of big government" over. By 2011, Clinton reversed himself, declaring that it was government's role to "give people the tools and create the conditions to make the most of our lives."

So what happened?

Capitalism failed to make a case for itself. Back in 1998, shortly after the world seemed to reach a consensus on the ineffectiveness of socialist schemes, economists Daniel Yergin and Joseph Stanislaw wrote that the free market required something beyond mere success: It required "legitimacy." But, said Yergin and Stanislaw, "a system that takes the pursuit of self-interest and profit as its guiding light does not necessarily satisfy the yearning in the human soul for belief and some higher meaning beyond materialism." In other words, they wrote, while Spanish communists would die with the word "Stalin" on their lips, "few people would die with the words 'free markets' on their lips."

The failure to make a moral case for capitalism has doomed capitalism to the status of a perennial backup plan. When people are desperate or wealthy, they turn to socialism; only when they have no other alternative do they embrace the free market. After all, lies about guaranteed security are far more seductive than lectures about personal responsibility.

So what is the moral case for capitalism? It lies in recognition that socialism isn't a great idea gone wrong -- it's an evil philosophy in action. It isn't driven by altruism; it's driven by greed and jealousy. Socialism states that you owe me something simply because I exist. Capitalism, by contrast, results in a sort of reality-forced altruism: I may not want to help you, I may dislike you, but if I don't give you a product or service you want, I will starve. Voluntary exchange is more moral than forced redistribution. Socialism violates at least three of the Ten Commandments: It turns government into God, it legalizes thievery and it elevates covetousness. Discussions of income inequality, after all, aren't about prosperity but about petty spite. Why should you care how much money I make, so long as you are happy?

Conservatives talk results when discussing the shortcomings of socialism. They're right: Socialism is ineffective, destructive and stunting to the human spirit. But they're wrong to abandon the field of morality when discussing the contrast between freedom and control. And it's this abandonment -- this perverse laziness -- that has led to socialism's comeback, even though within living memory, we have seen continental economies collapse and millions slaughtered in the name of this false god.

Negotiating With Space Nazis

January 15, 2014

On Tuesday, the Iranian government announced that it had reached a secret agreement with the West on its nuclear development. The details of the agreement were not released, but suffice it to say that the Iranians could not contain their glee. Iranian President Hassan Rouhani celebrated the deal with an English-language tweet claiming that the "world powers surrendered to Iranian nation's will"; Iranian Army Commander Maj. Gen. Ataollah Salehi said the diplomatic breakthrough resulted from American military "weakness"; and the Iranian foreign minister laid a wreath at the tomb of the Beirut Marine barracks bomber.

Meanwhile, President Barack Obama urged the United States Congress to "give peace a chance." After weeks of sending out his pacifist minions, including faux pro-Israel group J Street, to tell Americans that support for sanctions meant support for war, Obama himself echoed that message. "My preference is for peace and diplomacy," the apparent flower-child-in-chief stated. "And this is one of the reasons why I've sent the message to Congress that now is not the time for us to impose new sanctions. Now is the time for us to allow the diplomats and technical experts to do their work." He said that a rational, reasonable Iran would be "willing to walk through the door of opportunity that's presented to them."

Only Iran is not rational or reasonable. It is delusionally anti-Western and anti-Semitic, which means that America is now in negotiations not just with a terror-supporting state but radicals with more than a hint of insanity.

To prove this point, on Sunday, the Iranian semiofficial news agency FARS, which bills itself as independent but is effectively regime-run, ran a news article explaining that since the end of World War II, America had been run by a shadow government of Nazi space aliens. Seriously.

Basing its report on documents supposedly culled from National Security Agency leaker Edward Snowden, FARS reported that there was no "incontrovertible proof" that the American foreign policy agenda was driven by an "alien/extraterrestrial intelligence agenda."

Not "alien" as in foreigner. "Alien" as in little green men from Mars. FARS quotes Snowden as stating that there "were actually two governments in the U.S., one that was elected, and the other, secret regime, governing in the dark." This shadow regime had been run by space aliens -- also known as "Tall Whites" -- who were operating their regime from Nevada after emigrating from Nazi Germany after World War II. These space aliens, FARS stated, built the Nazi war machine's submarines.

This would be hilarious were it not part of a piece. Large swaths of the Islamic world also buy the myth that Jews use the blood of non-Jewish children in both their Passover matza and Purim hamentashen. "The Protocols of the Elders of Zion" remains a bestseller throughout the Islamic world. Iranian television routinely broadcasts Holocaust denial, while Iranian press outlets proclaim that the Zionist regime is producing another Hitler.

Assume for a moment that the Iranian regime actually believes the propaganda it spouts. Why, then, would it negotiate in good faith with space alien Nazis who drink Muslim blood?

Many pacifists in the West, including Obama, apparently assume that no one rational would continue to develop nuclear weapons in the face of world opposition, especially when offered a way out. What Obama fails to recognize is that Iran is far from rational -- and, more importantly, Obama's own assumptions about Iranian intentions put America and the West in a position of weakness. This weakness will be on display for all the world to see when Iran goes nuclear.

Abortion and the Suicide of the West

January 22, 2014

Jenelle Evans, 22, had an abortion this year. Originally featured on MTV four years ago as a pregnant teenager, Evans, who loves to party, had a son, gave the son to her mother to raise, got into heroin, got married and went to jail; her husband ended up in jail as well on drug charges. They got divorced. He didn't know that Evans was pregnant. She got an abortion. He found out about it on the commercials for "Teen Mom 2."

Now she's pregnant again. With a third guy. Who may or may not be seeing another woman on the side.

Since the legally and morally despicable decision of the Supreme Court in Roe v. Wade in 1973, American women have aborted some 56 million children. The vast majority of these children have been aborted for reasons that have nothing to do with rape, incest or the health of the mother. We have destroyed an entire generation of children purely for self-worship. Children are difficult; therefore, they can be done away with. Children are burdensome; therefore, they don't exist in the womb. Or, as President Barack Obama once put it regarding his own daughters, "If they make a mistake, I don't want them punished with a baby."

Meanwhile, the same society that has busily anesthetized millions to the murder of the unborn casually pushes social costs onto the next generation -- a generation that, increasingly, does not exist. According to the 2010 census, just 24 percent of the American population is under age 18, compared with 39.4 percent that is 45 and older. America is aging, and aging quickly.

And what of the young? Their chief concerns these days are legalization of marijuana, state-sponsored same-sex marriage and provision of birth control. If we think the demographics and economics of the country look bad now, wait until America relies on a generation of overprivileged, underachieving Americans convinced of their own moral rectitude based on a puerile libertarianism freed of libertarianism's consequences. Sex and drugs have replaced building for the future; abortion and the welfare state have replaced consequences.

In the end, this philosophy will lead to the dominance of the state. There are only two types of society that can survive. First, there is the heavy-entitlement, heavily regulated society, in which compulsion takes the place of free choice. Second, there is the free society, in which individual actions carry individual consequences. America used to be the second type of society. As we realize that there is no next generation to foot our bills, we will transition more toward the first.

So, how can we solve all of this? Not through the law -- the law follows culture. The only way to restore an American future is to restore the social and religious institutions that fostered genuine American values. This means fighting back against the tyranny of those who conveniently proclaim to "live and let live" while simultaneously demanding that Americans with traditional values shut the hell up. This means emboldening our churches and synagogues to once again speak out on behalf of virtue. This means treating family as a priority rather than an afterthought or punishment.

Evans is a victim of the society that built her -- a society that has enabled her misdeeds and rewarded her sins. But she cannot be the basis of America's future. If she is, America will, quite literally, have no future.

How Hollywood Is Killing
Same-Sex Marriage

January 29, 2014

In May 2012, Vice President Joe Biden floated a political trial balloon: He came out in favor of same-sex marriage. In the process, he stated that the way had been paved for the same-sex marriage movement by Hollywood. "I think 'Will & Grace' probably did more to educate the American public than almost anything anybody's ever done so far." Biden, of course, was absolutely right: Hollywood's personalization of the societal issue of same-sex marriage has shifted millions of minds.

Now, unfortunately for same-sex marriage advocates, Hollywood is busily shifting those minds back.

On Sunday, the Grammys tooted its self-proclaimed righteousness by trotting out Queen Latifah to officiate the mass wedding of 33 couples, including gay couples. She did so as new Grammy winner Macklemore shouted cloyingly sanctimonious antireligious slogans into his microphone: "The right-wing conservatives think it's a decision / And you can be cured with some treatment and religion ... Playing God, aw nah, here we go / America the brave still fears what we don't know / And God loves all his children is somehow forgotten / But we paraphrase a book written 3,500 years ago." To top off the marriages, Madonna then staggered out to warble "Open Your Heart."

This wasn't an argument for same-sex marriage. It wasn't even attractive image-making on behalf of same-sex marriage. It was hatred of Biblical values cloaked in pietistic nonsense.

Begin with the marriages themselves. The only rationale for getting married on the Grammys en masse would be either attention-seeking or spite toward Americans with traditional values, or both. Neither of these rationales scream "love," "commitment" or "societal building block."

Move on to the cheering audience -- a group of anti-marriage Hollywoodites who largely see the institution itself as patriarchal. The same folks standing up for same-sex marriage at the Grammys largely scorn the institution of marriage itself. The only time they embrace marriage is when it is being mocked, undermined or perverted. That's not a cuddly case for same-sex marriage.

Finally, look at the artists: Macklemore, who rages against religious Americans for cash and Grammys; Madonna, who is happy to glom onto the marriage bandwagon after selling her body for decades, and running through a raft of unsuccessful marriages and relationships of her own; Queen Latifah, acting as a stand-in for the government, offering up salvation via paper licenses from the state. None of this warms hearts or changes minds.

But this is Hollywood unmasked: angry, vindictive, self-righteous, anti-Biblical. The case for same-sex marriage rests on an application of Biblical principle -- monogamy and commitment -- to actions condemned by Biblical text. For years, Hollywood was able to get away with perverting the Bible by ignoring it. But in its rush to congratulate itself for overthrowing Biblical values without a shot, Hollywood spiked the football and revealed its true agenda. And that agenda is not the agenda of tolerance for individuals, but an ugly agenda of unearned moral superiority via destruction of traditional values.

Letter to My Newborn Daughter

February 5, 2014

Last Tuesday evening at 6:19 p.m. PST, my wife gave birth to our first child, a 7-pound, 9-ounce, 21-inch little girl named Leeya Eliana. The labor was long, approximately 26 hours, and my wife endured it heroically. Before, we were a married couple; now, we are a family.

On the sixth day of her life, I wrote my little girl a letter to memorialize our hopes for her at the dawn of her life. With my wife's permission, here it is:

Dear Leeya Eliana,

This is Daddy and Mommy writing to you. You are now six days old, and you are tiny and cute, and you poop a lot -- and you get really mad when anybody tries to change you. But you are also sweet and calm, and you look at us with your huge blue-gray eyes, and we love you so much because we know that not only are you a manifestation of how much Mommy and Daddy love each other, but you are the future of the Jewish people and the American people, and that we are preserving God's word and His freedom for the next generations. That's why we gave you your name: Leeya -- in Hebrew, "I Belong To God."

And you were our answer, Leeya. After Mommy and Daddy prayed very hard to Hashem to give them a healthy little baby, God answered them: Eliana. So your first name is about your relationship with God, and your middle name is about how thankful we are for you.

We hope you grow up to be the best, most principled, most joyful person in the entire world. We want you to be a leader for God, no matter what you choose to do -- to live with His justice and

His compassion, with His standards and His kindness. And we want you to love your family as much as we love you, and to carry forward our mission as a family and as a people. We will do our best to train and guide you. We promise to always take you seriously and to always listen to you. And we promise to never leave you.

You are the best thing that has ever happened to us, and that's what makes all the poop and the crying and the late night feedings and the sleep deprivation worth it. You may not always agree with everything we do -- you're going to be a teenager, and you're going to realize that Daddy and Mommy are just human beings trying their best. But we will do our best to ensure that you understand that we love you more than anything, and that it is our mission to help you find the best path to serving God.

Love you forever,
Daddy and Mommy

Why Democrats Hate Work

February 12, 2014

Last week, the Congressional Budget Office released a report discussing the ramifications of Obamacare. The report revealed that the work-hour equivalent of approximately 2.5 million jobs would disappear from the workforce, thanks to Obamacare, in a voluntary process in which employees would simply dump out of their jobs, knowing they could get health care through expanded Medicaid and federal subsidies they would lose by working.

Sen. Charles Schumer, D-N.Y., an ideological leftist thought leader, spun the report as a massive positive for Obamacare: "The single mom, who's raising three kids (and) has to keep a job because of health care, can now spend some time raising those kids. That's a family value." And Senate Majority Leader Harry Reid, D-Nev., celebrated the report as a defeat for the dreaded condition known as "job lock" -- the situation in which you have to stick at a job you don't like for the benefits. "We have the CBO report," Reid stated, "which rightfully says, that people shouldn't have job lock. If they -- we live in a country where there should be free agency. People can do what they want."

But, of course, people can only do what they want by taxing other Americans, borrowing from foreign creditors, and burdening future generations with unsustainable debt. And unfortunately, Schumer's proclamation that the greatest beneficiaries of Obamacare will be single mothers turns out to be false: One of the studies relied upon by the CBO stated that those who benefit from the end of job lock are disproportionately white, single and of work age.

In reality, the Democratic vision of the world centers on the notion that work itself is a great evil to be avoided, and that any program allowing people to free themselves of work -- whether to finger-paint or start a garage band -- is an unmitigated good. "Job lock," according to the definition Reid gives, goes by another name, according to those who live in the real world: "having a job." There are times that everyone hates his or her job. Were they freed from the economic consequences of having these jobs, they'd drop out of the workforce.

There are only two problems with this strategy: First, someone has to pay for it; second, it is not the recipe for human fulfillment. Leisure time is only leisure time when it is earned; otherwise, leisure time devolves into soul-killing lassitude. There's a reason so many new retirees, freed from the treadmill of work, promptly keel over on the golf course: Work fulfills us. It keeps us going.

This doesn't mean every job fulfills us, naturally. But we have all worked rotten jobs in order to get to jobs we like. Capitalism doesn't mean, as my grandmother used to say, that you don't have to walk through some manure to get to the roses. It just means that if you walk through enough manure, you'll likely get to the roses sooner or later. In the leisure-first world of the left, however, wallowing in mire is a preferred road to happiness over the hard work that brings true fulfillment.

The European style of living is seductive: fewer hours worked, more hours at the cafe, less concern over self-betterment. But that style of living does not produce a purposeful life. Perhaps we'd all be happier in the short run were we somehow freed of our job lock. But we certainly would not contribute to the betterment of ourselves or the community around us. We'd leave the world worse than we found it. The opt-out society opts us out of societal happiness.

The Left Preaches the Great Apocalypse of Global Warming

February 19, 2014

This week, Secretary of State John Kerry announced to a group of Indonesian students that global warming was "perhaps the world's most fearsome weapon of mass destruction." He added, "Because of climate change, it's no secret that today Indonesia is ... one of the most vulnerable countries on Earth. It's not an exaggeration to say that the entire way of life that you live and love is at risk."

Meanwhile, Hollywood prepared to drop a new blockbuster based on the biblical story of Noah. The film, directed by Darren Aronofsky, centers on the story of the biblical character who built an ark after God warned him that humanity would be destroyed thanks to its sexual immorality and violent transgressions. The Hollywood version of the story, however, has God punishing humanity not for actual sin, but for overpopulation and global warming -- an odd set of sins, given God's express commandments in Genesis 1:28 to "be fruitful, multiply, fill the earth, and subdue it."

This weird perspective on sin -- the notion that true sin is not sin, but that consumerism is -- is actually nothing new. In the 1920s, the left warned of empty consumerism with the fire and brimstone of Jonathan Edwards; Sinclair Lewis famously labeled the American middle class "Babbitts" -- characters who cared too much about buying things.

In his novel of the same name, Lewis sneered of his bourgeois antihero, "He had enormous and poetic admiration, though very little understanding, of all mechanical devices. They were his symbols of truth and beauty." Lewis wrote, through the voice of his radical character Doane, that consumerism has created "standardization of thought, and of course, the traditions of competition. The real villains of the piece are the clean, kind, industrious Family Men who use every known brand of trickery and cruelty to insure the prosperity of their cubs. The worst thing about these fellows it that they're so good and, in their work at least, so intelligent."

Lewis, of course, was a socialist. So were anti-consumerism compatriots like H.G. Wells, H.L. Mencken and Herbert Croly. And their brand of leftism was destined to infuse the entire American left over the course of the 20th century. As Fred Siegel writes in his new book, "The Revolt Against The Masses," this general feeling pervaded the left during the 1950s, even as more Americans were attending symphony concerts than ballgames, with 50,000 Americans per year buying paperback version of classics. That's because if the left were to recognize the great power of consumerism in bettering lives and enriching culture, the left would have to become the right.

Of course, consumerism is not an unalloyed virtue. Consumerism can be utilized for hedonism. But it can also be utilized to make lives better, offering more opportunity for spiritual development. It's precisely this latter combination that the left fears, because if consumerism and virtue are allied, there is no place left for the Marxist critique of capitalism -- namely that capitalism makes people less compassionate, more selfish, and ethically meager. And so consumerism must be severed from virtue (very few leftists critique Americans' propensity for spending cash on Lady Gaga concerts) so that it can be castigated as sin more broadly.

In a world in which consumerism is the greatest of all sins, America is the greatest of all sinners, which, of course, is the point of the anti-consumerist critique from the left: to target America. Global warming represents the latest apocalyptic consequence threatened by the leftist gods for the great iniquity of buying things, developing products, and competing in the global marketplace. And America must be called to heel by the great preachers in Washington, D.C., and Hollywood.

Piers Morgan Is the American Left

February 26, 2014

This week, CNN's Piers Morgan announced that "Piers Morgan Live" would be coming to an ignominious end sometime in March. His replacement has not yet been chosen. But his television demise came not a moment too soon for millions of Americans who had tired of his sneering nastiness.

The New York Times chose not to see it that way. Instead, the Times insisted, Morgan's problem sprang from his British accent and heritage: "Old hands in the television news business suggest that there are two things a presenter cannot have: an accent or a beard ... Mr. Morgan is clean shaven and handsome enough, but there are tells in his speech -- the way he says the president's name for one thing (Ob-AA-ma) -- that suggest that he is not from around here." Morgan himself attributed his downfall to his foreignness: "Look, I am a British guy debating American cultural issues, including guns, which has been very polarizing, and there is no doubt that there are many in the audience who are tired of me banging on about it."

No doubt the notion of a British entertainer coming to America, clearing millions of dollars, and then lecturing Americans on their fundamental rights galled many. But what truly galled so many Americans was Morgan's underlying perspective -- a perspective shared by the Times, as well as most of the left. Morgan, unfortunately, believes that Americans are typically racist, sexist, homophobic bigots clinging to guns without regard to the safety of children. We, in his world of unearned moral superiority, are the bad guys.

Which is why Morgan had nothing to say when I appeared on his program in the aftermath of the Sandy Hook Elementary massacre, handed him a copy of the Constitution to remind him of the Second Amendment, and then told him that he was a "bully ... demoniz(ing) people who differ from you politically by standing on the graves of the children of Sandy Hook." His only response: "How dare you."

It's why Morgan had nothing to say when I suggested a few months later that his gushing response to gay basketball player Jason Collins' coming out sprang from his disdain for the American people: "Why do you hate America so much that you think it's such a homophobic country, that when Jason Collins comes out it is the biggest deal in the history of humanity, and President Obama has to personally congratulate him?" Again, Morgan had no answer.

As the left has no answer. The left's perspective on the role of government is inextricably linked to its view that Americans, free of government strictures, are brutally discriminatory, selfishly violent. Without the guiding hand of our betters, we would all be Bull Connors (a government employee), hoses at the ready. Without the sage wisdom of our leftist superiors, we would all be shooting each other at shopping malls.

The countervailing perspective -- that America is a pretty damn great place filled with pretty damn great people -- has little currency for the left. But when their hate-Americans perspective is repeatedly exposed, Americans begin to find it tiresome. That's what happened with Morgan. That's what will happen to the American left if the American right somehow finds the stomach to call out the left's snobby scorn for everyday Americans.

The Faculty Lounge Administration

March 5, 2014

On Sunday, Secretary of State John Kerry appeared on CBS's "Face the Nation" to respond to Russia's invasion of the Crimea region of Ukraine. "You just don't in the 21st century behave in 19th century fashion by invading another country on completely trumped up pretext," Kerry stated. He added, "It's an incredible act of aggression. It is really a stunning, willful choice by President (Vladimir) Putin to invade another country."

So, what would the United States do about Russian aggression? America would consider dropping its scheduled attendance at the G8 meeting in Sochi, Kerry said: "He is not going to have a Sochi G8, he may not even remain in the G8 if this continues." And on Monday, the Obama administration got truly tough: It announced that it would not send a presidential delegation to the Paralympic Winter Games in Sochi.

Which, of course, had Putin quaking in his boots. Because if there's one thing a Russian autocrat fears, it's faculty lounge-style sneering about his unsophistication followed by symbolic withdrawals from meaningless events.

But this sums up the Obama administration in its entirety: When it comes to dealing with America's enemies, the Obama White House simply assumes that there is no true conflict. After all, who could disagree with an America that has spent five years on bended knee to the rest of the world, that has minimized its influence in the world, and that is planning to slash its military by 30 percent over the next several years? Who could oppose an administration so dedicated to harmony that it is willing to undercut its own allies for the sake of a humbler America on the global stage?

This complete incapacity to understand America's geopolitical enemies dominated the 2012 election cycle. With the help of the media, the Obama campaign scoffed its way to victory by tut-tutting Mitt Romney's designation of Russia as America's chief geopolitical challenge. That acidic jeering, which cloaks a pathetic naivete, underscored America's unwillingness to place armed troops in Benghazi.

And that same desperate and ironical urbanity reared its ugly head last week when National Security Adviser Susan Rice blithely informed David Gregory, "It's nobody's interest to see violence return and the situation escalate." When Gregory asked whether Putin sees the world "in a Cold War context," Rice ignored the question entirely: "He may, but if he does, that's a pretty dated perspective."

But that's the point: If Obama and his staff disagree with a perspective, that doesn't mean it isn't real. Wishful thinking won't make the Palestinians an Israeli peace partner, no matter how much President Barack Obama pressures Israel to make concessions; caustically mocking Putin's worldview won't make it any less real or mitigate the Russian threat.

In the ivory tower inhabited by the great intellects of the Obama administration, however, no problem is too big to be thought or talked or surrendered away. If Russia won't change its perspective, we will simply cut our military more to convince them we mean well; if the Palestinians or Iranians don't change their perspectives, we will force Israel to negotiate with them in order to prove our goodwill.

Meanwhile, our enemies laugh. And they should. The global battlefield is no place for the Kennedy School political science grad students who inhabit our White House and believe that a well-aimed, snooty barb is a substitute for a muscular foreign policy presence.

The Entertainment President

March 12, 2014

For years, conservatives have puzzled over President Barack Obama's continued personal popularity in the face of his dramatically uninspiring performance as commander-in-chief. Obama seems to inspire a bizarre personal loyalty among his advocates, particularly among young people who should by all rights be concerned with their fading futures and collapsing prospects. Why do his numbers remain so stubbornly mediocre?

The answer came Tuesday in the form of a ridiculous video cut by Obama with the help of "The Hangover" star Zach Galifianakis and the online outlet Funny or Die. Funny or Die is in the viral video business; it often features celebrities in bizarre skits designed to draw clicks. But Funny or Die also has a political agenda: In September, the Los Angeles Times reported that Funny or Die honcho Mike Farah had become an integral part of "the campaign to ensure the success of President Obama's healthcare law." Obama enlisted Farah in July 2013 during a meeting with Hollywood bigwigs in which Obama recruited his arts team to rally to the Obamacare cause.

The video, the latest in an ongoing series of episodes of a faux talk show titled "Between Two Ferns," has Galifianakis interviewing Obama about Obamacare. The portly actor, best known for playing a moron in movies, asks Obama questions about whether he will miss winning at basketball when he is no longer president. Obama, on script, answers by getting testy with Galifianakis before pushing Obamacare with his usual lack of verve: "Healthcare.gov works great now. And millions of Americans have already gotten health care plans. And what we want is for people to know that you can get affordable health care."

That wasn't Obama's only major media appearance this week. Obama also introduced the Fox reboot of the miniseries "Cosmos," explaining to Americans that hope and change could still be attained through science: "America has always been a nation of fearless explorers who dream big and reach farther than others might imagine." Which sounds better than "America has always been a nation of close-minded bigots requiring the intervention of government to force them into tolerance and diversity."

Obama's pop-cultural focus may seem demeaning to the office of the presidency. It may be mockable. But it is also tremendously effective. In the first 24 hours alone, the "Between Two Ferns" segment received almost 8 million views; approximately 20,000 people visited Healthcare.gov directly from the watching the segment. That's not bad for a pure propaganda effort.

Conservatives must understand that culture is the lifeblood of politics. Most Republicans have no idea what Funny or Die is, let alone why people watch it. BuzzFeed is a dirty word to most conservatives, even though their sons and daughters read it regularly for its cat lists -- and some of them stay for the leftist politics. Obama gets culture, or at least does a serviceable job of pretending he does. His shock troops in the entertainment industry are willing to do the rest on behalf of the Obama agenda.

Why No One Minds His Own Business Anymore

March 19, 2014

When I was a kid -- which wasn't that long ago, given that I just turned 30 in January -- I recall hearing a popular phrase on the playground: "Mind your own business." MYOB reared its head whenever somebody threatened to rat out a fellow student for anything from harmless roughhousing to juvenile delinquency. The phrase is sometimes attributed to the First Epistle to the Thessalonians, a rough translation of which states: " ... make it your ambition to lead a quiet life: You should mind your own business and work with your hands, just as we told you, so that your daily life may win the respect of outsiders and so that you will not be dependent on anybody."

Unfortunately, the phrase "mind your own business" has lost all meaning. After all, you don't get to mind your own business in America today. If you're a religious business owner, the government can force you to serve a same-sex wedding and cover your employees' abortion-inclusive health care plan. If you're a landowner, the government can simply seize your property and hand it over to another private party in order to increase tax revenue. If you're an entrepreneur, the thicket of government intervention weighing you down, from minimum wage to tax regulation, stifles innovation and stymies creativity.

Today, Americans are only told to mind our own business when we're not, in fact, engaging in business. Concerned about the societal fallout from sexual promiscuity? Mind your own business. Worried about the rise of single motherhood? Mind your own business. Upset about an epidemic of young people seemingly willing to trade the responsibilities of adulthood for an infantilized freedom? Mind your own business.

Societal problems are now personal; personal problems are now societal.

That shift in the American mindset reflects a deeper shift in the nature of our relationship with government and each other. This week, Michelle Obama released a video explaining to us that we needed to sign up for Obamacare now -- for the sake of our mothers. "We nag you because we love you," the First Lady said.

But, of course, she doesn't love us. She doesn't even know us. Nonetheless, too many Americans have been convinced that individuals exercising personal choice are a societal problem; government, our Great Mother, can care for us personally. If we believe, as Hillary Clinton does, that it takes a village, then those who insist on personal privacy and freedom are obstacles to happiness and accomplishment. Only the collective is good. Any manifestation of individuality that poses a threat to that collective is by necessity evil.

We no longer live in a nation in which we can mind our own business. My business is your business, and vice versa -- unless, that is, we are engaged in activity that tears down family, church and community. If I'm a business owner rejecting service to a same-sex wedding, I have no right to invoke "mind your own business." Conversely, if I'm a member of a same-sex couple, I can invoke "mind your own business" all day long -- even if I'm making my business your business by engaging your services.

The obliteration of the distinction between the personal and the collective marks the end of American rights. But if you're worried about it, you should probably mind your own business.

Time for Congress to Telecommute

March 26, 2014

Few Americans have ever met their Congresspeople. They don't see them at the grocery store; they don't meet them at the bowling alley. They're more likely to see their representatives in photographs from the Daily Grill in Washington, D.C., than at a local town hall. Constituents' closest contact with those they elect comes on Election Day, when they punch a chad next to a name.

This is precisely the opposite of how government was supposed to work.

In Federalist No. 46, James Madison posited that members of Congress would "generally be favorable to the States" from which they sprang, rather than toward the federal government. The federal government had to be part-time, given the distances between the states and the time required to travel. Politicians generally ended up in Washington, D.C., for just a few years in the early days of the Republic. That part-time government led to smaller government. Representatives showed up to vote on issues of major import to their constituents; then they went home to live among those who voted for them.

With the dramatic increase in ease of transportation and the incredible decrease in the amount of time required to travel between far-flung areas of the United States, representatives began spending more and more time in Washington and less and less time in their home districts. The first session of Congress, which lasted from March 4, 1789, to March 3, 1791, ran a grand total of 519 days. During the 109th Congress, lasting from Jan. 4, 2005, to Dec. 8, 2006, Congress was in session for a whopping 692 days.

And Congresspeople spent more of that time in D.C. Many Congresspeople spend their weeks in Washington and fly home on weekends, if that often. Approximately eight in 10 Congresspeople spend more than 40 weekends per year in their districts, according to the Congressional Management Foundation and the Society for Human Resource Management.

This has a predictable impact: Congresspeople do not fear their constituents. They simply don't see them often enough to fear them. That's why Democrats crammed through Obamacare in the dead of night over the Christmas holiday -- they hoped to escape the wrath of their constituents. Members of Congress have more in common with the people they hobnob in Washington, D.C., than they do with the people they're supposed to represent.

But now there's an easy solution: telecommuting. Why should Congresspeople have to visit D.C.? Thanks to Skype, meetings are possible across the country. Thanks to email, communications are simple. And we've had the technology to vote from afar for decades. Why should we have backroom deals made over cigars thousands of miles distant from those who are affected by those deals? Instead, let's put Congresspeople among those who must choose them -- and let's let them live with the consequences of their decision-making.

If Washington is the problem, then telecommuting could be the solution. It's time to make our representatives answerable to their communities rather than their dinner buddies. And the way to do that is to keep them close, rather than allowing them to roam free with our tax dollars far from home.

Why Hillary Clinton Will Win in 2016

April 2, 2014

On Tuesday, House Budget Committee Chairman Paul Ryan, R-Wis., presented his 2015 budget proposal. The Senate Democrats did not provide any such proposal; President Barack Obama's proposal posited an unending federal deficit and massive tax increases. Ryan's proposal, by contrast, lowered the rate of increase of spending moderately (by $5.1 trillion over the next decade), struck Obamacare from the rolls, and suggested revamps to Social Security and Medicare.

This was possibly the dumbest thing Ryan could have done.

Senate Majority Leader Harry Reid, D-Nev., immediately jumped on the budget proposal, suggesting that Ryan's budget came from "Kochtopia," and that it had been produced in reality by the nefarious Koch brothers. The former Clinton administration secretary of labor called the budget "cruel and unusual punishment." Ryan, Democrats claimed, was mean, nasty, heartless, brutal.

The same day Ryan laid out his blueprint for spending, Obama and his minions claimed victory for Obamacare, trumpeting their fudged sign-up numbers for the Affordable Care Act. "7.1 million Americans have now signed up for private insurance plans through these market places! 7.1! Yep!" Obama blustered. Never mind the fact that Obama had canceled some 5 million health care plans and then threatened people with fines for failing to repurchase under Obamacare; never mind the fact that the administration would not release numbers on how many Americans had paid for Obamacare; never mind that well under 1 million Americans who previously lacked health insurance took advantage of the Obamacare exchanges to get into the market. Obama had wanted his 7 million; now he had his 7 million.

Republicans reacted with predictable confusion and outrage. They suggested -- rightly -- that Obama had "cooked the books." They complained that sign-up numbers did not justify the entire overthrow of the health insurance system. And Obama, the man who canceled plans, doctors and drugs for millions of Americans, responded thusly: "Why are folks working so hard for people not to have health insurance?"

This is why Republicans will lose in 2016.

Democrats understand the art of narrative. Republicans do not. Republicans would rather have Ryan wave around a 100-page budget backed by all the stats. Democrats would rather point at Ryan and say he hates children. Americans don't have time to read 100-page budgets. Case closed.

Republicans would rather complain about each and every aspect of Obamacare. They enjoy debunking Obama's falsified statistics and singling out his corruption of data. Democrats would prefer to point at those Republicans and suggest that they don't care enough about poor, sick children. Americans don't have time to wade through media falsehoods or read beyond the headlines. Case closed.

In 2016, the Democratic Party will nominate Hillary Clinton. Her narrative has already been written by the media: starry-eyed young Republican turned disenchanted leftist seeking honesty and accountability in government; wronged woman married to a charming rogue, victimized by a viciously sexist right-wing conspiracy; first lady, senator, jet-setting secretary of state; elderly grandmother called once more to public service by her ailing country. You can all but hear the music swell and the slow clap begin as she steps to the microphone.

What, precisely, is the Republican narrative? Is it Ryan's CPA-style approach to government management? Is it Chris Christie's government-as-huggable-friend Hurricane Sandy routine? Is it Jeb Bush's riches-to-riches story?

Republicans continue to lose because Republicans get distracted from story by information. Democrats continue to win because they never let information get in the way of a good story. Until

Republicans figure that simple truth out, no amount of truth will put a Republican back in the Oval Office.

The Rise of American Totalitarianism

April 9, 2014

Last Thursday, Mozilla, the company that's home to the web browser Firefox, forced the resignation of CEO Brendan Eich. What, precisely, had Eich done wrong? Back in 2008, Eich had donated $1,000 to the Proposition 8 effort backing traditional marriage in California. Dating website OKCupid posted a ban on Firefox traffic, issuing a message to Firefox users instead: "Those who seek to deny love and instead enforce misery, shame, and frustration are our enemies, and we wish them nothing but failure." That ban reportedly prompted the action at Mozilla.

Of course, it was the people pushing for Eich's ouster who were enforcing "misery, shame, and frustration." Eich had never brought his politics into the workplace. Mozilla had no history of treating homosexuals differently, and no single instance of Eich doing so could be documented. Nonetheless, he had violated the dictates of the Thought Police. And thus he was ousted.

It's a disturbing story, to be sure. But it's also just the tip of the iceberg: Unfortunately, the same folks administering the private Thought Police would love to extend their control into the realm of government. These are not libertarians arguing for the right to hire and fire as you see fit in the private market. These are power brokers seeking to use whatever means necessary to quash opposition.

That's why gay couples have sued photographers, bakeries and florist shops, attempting to shut them down if they refuse to cater to same-sex weddings. That's why the Obama administration has attempted to fine businesses that do not wish to pay for health coverage they deem sinful. The underlying idea: If the left dislikes what you do, the left can compel you not to do it. As Kevin

Williamson of National Review writes, American society is quickly morphing into a system governed by T.H. White's totalitarian principle: "Everything not forbidden is compulsory."

Freedom is secondary to the yays and nays of the governing few in this vision. Freedom is merely that which the government allows -- and the government should only allow you to do the bidding of the left. If you, recognizing that sometimes people will take action with which you disagree, believe that government should stay out of people's business, you must therefore be an advocate for discrimination and brutality. To allow Eich to work is to discriminate against gays. To allow religious businesses to reject contraceptive mandates is to push women into back alley abortions. Forget the notion of disagreeing with your opinion, but defending your right to say it -- in the view of the leftist totalitarians, such a notion is inherently unworkable.

When fascism comes, it will come not with jackboots but with promises of a better world. The jackboots come later, when we've all been shamed into silence -- when we've been taught that to allow that with which we disagree is to agree with it, and when we've accepted that the best method of preventing such disagreement is government power. We're on the verge. All it will take is the silence of good people -- people on all sides of the political aisle -- who fall prey to the ultimate temptation in a republic: the temptation to force their values on others utilizing the machinery of government. We're already more than halfway there.

Why Conservatives Win Elections and Lose the War

April 16, 2014

On April 1, 2014, President Barack Obama triumphantly announced that 7.1 million Americans had selected a health insurance plan through Obamacare. In doing so, he nastily labeled his political opposition uncaring and unfeeling. "Why are folks working so hard for people not to have health insurance?" Obama asked. "Why are they so mad about the idea of people having health insurance?"

That night, Comedy Central's Stephen Colbert sat behind his desk at "The Colbert Report," playing his version of a conservative: vicious, mean and cruel. "I wish I could come to you with some good news, but the worst imaginable thing has happened: Millions of Americans are going to get health care."

This is why conservatives lose. They lose because while they proclaim that Obama's signature legislation fails on the merits, raising costs and lowering access to vital services, the left surges forth with a different message: Conservatives are rotten to the core.

This message doesn't just emanate from politicians in Washington. Entertainers like Colbert parrot back White House talking points in the guise of mockery. For many young people who get their news from Colbert, the only conservatism they see comes out of the mouth of a hard-core leftist playing a conservative who doesn't exist. There is no conservative sitting up nights wondering how to deprive Americans of health insurance. But many young people don't know that. They simply assume that the person Colbert is parodying must exist -- otherwise, his satire isn't satire at all, but a political smear job, an ugly and stereotypical blackfacing of conservatives.

For Colbert, to be funny, one of two alternatives must be true: Either his repulsive character must be based on a core reality -- conservatives are evil -- or his audience must believe in that core unreality. With the help of Obama and an entertainment industry dedicated full time to the defacing of conservatives' character, the latter has certainly become the case. Too many Americans now perceive conservatives as morally deficient. All it has cost is hundreds of millions of dollars and several decades of consistent attacks springing from Hollywood and the political world.

That's why so many Americans now seem comfortable giving the government power to violate freedom of conscience for conservatives: Evil people don't deserve freedom and therefore, can be deprived of it. People who consider themselves civil libertarians suddenly find their inner totalitarian when it comes to Christian-owned bakeries. That can only happen when those people become convinced that Christian-owned bakeries are fronts of hatred and darkness. And that can only happen when they are falsely maligned as such, over and over again.

Conservatives can win short-term political fights and lose the war for hearts and minds. And that's precisely what has happened, thanks to the lack of moral clarity on the right. It's not enough to be good on policy. Americans must think of you as good. By neglecting that deeper battle, conservatives sow the seeds of their own destruction -- and the destruction of American freedoms, as well.

Why Bundy Ranch Is Just the Beginning

April 23, 2014

This week, Nevada rancher Cliven Bundy, whose standoff with the federal government over taxes and land-use rights has captivated the nation, announced, "I don't believe I owe one penny to the United States government. I don't have a contract with the United States government." His legal case is problematic; the Bureau of Land Management certainly has jurisdiction over the federal lands on which his cattle graze. But his moral case is significantly stronger: paying taxes to a government that uses those tax dollars to restrict your activities on land your family has worked since the 19th century -- over a turtle, no less -- is sickening stuff. A government squeeze is a government squeeze.

Bundy's position on the federal government itself is unjustifiable. He stated in a recent interview: "I believe this is a sovereign state of Nevada. I abide by all of Nevada state laws. But I don't recognize the United States government as even existing." Obviously, the federal government does exist, and if the state of Nevada exists, it only does so because it was formed with the permission of the feds under the Constitution.

In fact, the Constitution of the of Nevada explicitly denies Bundy's interpretation of the law: "no power exists in the people of this or any other State of the Federal Union to dissolve their connection therewith or perform any act tending to impair, subvert, or resist the Supreme Authority of the government of the United States."

So Bundy's wrong on the legal and constitutional merits of his anti-federal case. But he does represent a growing problem in the

United States: the problem of a seemly omnipotent federal government running roughshod over local rights.

As America's federal government grows, and as its unelected bureaucracy extends its reach over nearly every aspect of American life, more and more Americans will justifiably believe that their government no longer represents them. They will show up to Bundy Ranch-type standoffs believing that the government is not their government.

When American colonists plotted revolt against the British government, they did so on the pretext that they were being taxed without representation. James Otis, the firebrand leader of the early anti-British movement, famously wrote: "no parts of His Majesty's dominions can be taxed without their consent ... every part has a right to be represented in the supreme or some subordinate legislature." But the simple reality was that the colonists likely would not have accepted representation in the Parliament as a justification for taxation; Congress stated in 1765 that the colonies "are not, and from their local Circumstances, cannot be, represented in the House of Commons of Great Britain." The impracticality of directing representatives thousands of miles away on complex legislation in a time without instant communication precluded the possibility of America becoming part of a British federation.

We have instant communication today, but a no more responsive government. Resistance to the Stamp Act killed its implementation in the United States but paved the way for war; resistance to the BLM's enforcement of federal law in the Bundy Ranch situation ended in federal withdrawal, but is merely the first step in a far-larger conflict. Like Bundy or not, his situation will not be the last of its kind, so long as the federal government insists on its ever-growing authority, and so long as states and localities refuse to stand up for their citizens.

Of Donald Sterling's Racism and the Rise of Thoughtcrime

April 30, 2014

In November 2009, Los Angeles Clippers owner Donald Sterling settled a lawsuit in which the Department of Justice alleged that Sterling had discriminated against Hispanics, blacks and families without children in his rental properties. The lawsuit contained testimony that Sterling had suggested Hispanics were poor tenants because they "smoke, drink, and just hang around the building," and that "black tenants smell and attract vermin." The settlement cost him and his insurers $2.73 million.

The NBA and the national media said virtually nothing. That same year, the NAACP gave him a Lifetime Achievement Award.

In 2005, Sterling signed a check for more than $5 million to settle a lawsuit alleging that he had attempted to prevent non-Koreans from renting in his facilities in Koreatown.

The NBA and the national media said virtually nothing.

This week, Sterling's 31-year-old girlfriend, V. Stiviano, released a tape of the 80-year-old racist being an 80-year-old racist. Sterling apparently told Stiviano he didn't want her posting pictures of black men on her Instagram account and didn't want her bringing black men to Clippers games.

The entire media establishment suddenly went insane. Colin Cowherd of ESPN idiotically called for the league to void all of Sterling's contracts with his players and agents -- a violation of basic contract law. Magic Johnson declared that the NBA should force Sterling to sell his team -- a violation of basic contract law. President Barack Obama, determined never to let an opportunity pass to label

America racist, took to the microphones to declare Sterling's racism a symptom of America's "legacy of race and slavery and segregation."

This is, at the very least, hypocrisy. Last year, Sterling signed coach Doc Rivers, who is black, to a contract worth $7 million per year. Chris Paul, who is black, is slated to make nearly $19 million this season. Blake Griffin, who is black, is slated to make $16 million. DeAndre Jordan will make $11 million. The coach, these players and their agents surely knew about Sterling's legacy. So did Cowherd, Johnson and Obama. They all said nothing.

But the big problem here isn't hypocrisy. The big problem is that the market is turning on Sterling not over action, but over words. Sterling's a pig, and that's been no secret for decades. But what triggered America's response?   Sterling's thoughts. American society now considers expression of thought to be significantly more important than action. Sterling got away with actual discrimination for years. But now he is caught on tape telling his gold-digging girlfriend he doesn't like blacks, and that's when the firestorm erupts?

This is the thought police at work. Feelings matter more than action. Words matter more than harming others. That sets a radically dangerous precedent for freedom of thought and speech, particularly for those whose thought and speech we hate. Freedom of speech and thought matters especially when it is speech and thought with which we disagree. The moment the majority decides to destroy people for engaging in thought it dislikes, thoughtcrime becomes a reality.

Sterling's career should have been ended by public outrage based on his established patterns of discrimination years ago. To end it based not on such disreputable action but on private musings caught on tape demonstrates America's newfound disregard for the rights of those whose thought we find despicable.

The Left's Phantom Wars

May 7, 2014

On Monday, as Vladimir Putin waged an actual war in Ukraine, Bashar Assad waged an actual war in Syria, and a Nigerian terror group waged an actual war on underage girls, President Barack Obama announced his own war on "climate disruption." White House adviser John Podesta explained on Monday afternoon that Obama would be acting alone to push new regulations under the Clean Air Act to combat climate change. That announcement came in the wake of an 840-page report from the federal government suggesting that the globe is on the verge of a meltdown: "Climate change, once considered an issue for a distant future, has moved firmly into the present."

That's hardly the only war in which the left is currently engaged. The left is fighting a war on racism -- a war in which the declared enemy is America, given that America is apparently plagued by "hidden bias." That's the newest term trotted out by MTV, which has launched its "look different" initiative, in coordination with shakedown groups like the Council on American-Islamic Relations, the NAACP, the National Council of La Raza and the Gay and Lesbian Alliance Against Defamation. The goal: to convince young people that while they aren't overtly racist, they hold secret racist beliefs that can only be cleansed by embracing the leftist agenda. The war must go on, after all, even if the enemy has been largely vanquished.

There's the left's phantom war on sexism, too, in which Democrats claim women are victimized by a male patriarchy. Women, leftists say, earn significantly less than men, despite studies showing that in most major cities, young women without children and with the same jobs as men earn significantly more. Women, leftists say, are victimized by a conservative religious minority that doesn't want to pay for their birth control. Again, the enemies of women remain faceless -- but we are told they lurk behind every corner. The winning strategy, once again: embrace leftism.

The war on poverty continues apace, as well. The latest incarnation: the war on income inequality -- a war specifically geared toward endlessness. After all, sans Communist revolution, income inequality will always exist. And according to the left, it will always require rectification.

Today's leftism tilts at windmills rather than fighting real opponents. It ignores actual conflict in favor of broader, amorphous battles with shapeless opponents and no clear measures of victory. After all, how will we know if we defeat climate change? There is no way to tell whether we did it, or whether the global temperature was set to drop anyway. How will we know if we defeat sexism? Clearly, the left believes that women in the workplace in record numbers and achievement of equal pay for equal work doesn't do the trick. How will we know if we defeat racism? The left has already moved the goalposts from equal opportunity to equal result, an unachievable pipe dream in the absence of totalitarian control.

And so the wars go on -- endless, expensive, draining. They sap America of our vitality, our strength and most importantly, our core values. But at least, the left tells us, we have gained heaven: an everlasting unearned moral superiority over our fellow nonracist, nonsexist, non-poverty-hating Americans.

How the West Won the Great Hashtag War of 2014

May 14, 2014

This week, a picture emerged of Islamist terror group Boko Haram's leader Abubakar Shekau holding a machine gun in one hand and a piece of paper in the other. On that paper was scrawled: "#WeSurrender."

Thus came to an end the Great Hashtag War of 2014.

Led by the bravery of First Lady Michelle Obama, former Secretary of State Hillary Clinton and the Democratic women of the United States Senate, the West tweeted Boko Haram into submission. When Obama released the H-bomb of twitter -- a sad duck-faced picture of herself in an empty room holding a sign reading #BringBackOurGirls -- total victory was achieved: 276 Nigerian girls who had been kidnapped and converted to Islam avoided sale into sex slavery, and the 150 Nigerians murdered by Boko Haram just last week suddenly sprang back to life.

No wonder the Obama State Department has saluted the Power of Hashtag. If only we'd discovered it earlier, we could have saved tens of millions of lives. If the French had only utilized the #MaginotLine instead of the Maginot Line, the Nazi jackboots never would have clip-clopped along the Champs-Elysees.

Now, there were those who argued that hashtagging by world leaders was not merely useless but counterproductive. They argued that hashtag foreign policy projected a sense of Western impotence combined with an overweening sense of unearned moral superiority that comes from sounding off in public. They said that when a former secretary of state neglected to label Boko Haram a terrorist group during her tenure, but tweeted out #BringBackOurGirls, that demonstrated the pathetic weakness of the Obama administration. They opined that it was one thing for powerless people in Nigeria to push a hashtag campaign in an attempt to prompt action from authorities, but quite another for the authorities themselves to ignore action in favor of hashtagging.

But that missed the point: Awareness was raised. People in authority demonstrated their outrage at kidnapping and sex slavery. Not enough to actually do anything useful, of course, but enough to publicly express that outrage. And now that we all know their feelings on the subject, we can go home happy.

As it turns out, the proper solution to a plea for help is to amplify that plea rather than to help. By doing so, awareness is raised, consciousness is increased, chakras are released. The Power of Hashtag reigns supreme.

The best news of all: You were there. You were part of the Hastag War. We will be thankful for that years from now, when we're sitting by the fireplace with our grandchildren on our knees, and they ask us what we did in the great Hashtag Wars, we won't have to cough, shift them to the other knee, and say, "Well, I tweeted about Solange and Jay-Z."

Will Detroit Be Healed by Searching for 'Subtle Racism'?

May 21, 2014

Just off of the James C. Lodge Freeway in Detroit is Eight Mile Road. The stretch near the freeway is just east of the famed area that provided the basis for the Eminem film of the same name. To its north lie predominantly white suburbs -- over 77 percent of those who live in Oakland County are white -- with median family income in excess of $65,000. Married couples comprise approximately half of households, with fewer than 15 percent of households led by a single female. Since 1990, the population of Oakland County has jumped from 1.083 million to 1.202 million.

South of Eight Mile Road lies the city of Detroit, with a nearly 83 percent black population and a median household income of under $27,000. Almost 74 percent of households in Detroit are led by single parents, nearly all women. The population of the city has dropped from 1.027 million in that same period to approximately 713,000.

Eight Mile Road itself paints a bleak picture. In the middle of a weekday, the streets are sparsely populated; old, solid-structure brick houses with rotten roofs dot the side streets; beaten-up Pontiacs from the early 1990s sitting forlornly in driveways. Hair salons, liquors stores and rim stores are open for business, but they're located between defunct hair stores, liquor stores and rim stores.

What happened in Detroit? Horrific governance destroyed the industrial infrastructure that created the growing mixed-population base of the city; it centralized employment in the government while devastating the business and tax base. Businesses fled to the suburbs, as did whites. The bulk of the black population, trapped in a cycle of poverty and government dependence, sold a bill of goods by Detroit's politicians, stayed behind. Those politicians covered their mismanagement with racially charged rhetoric, from former Mayor Coleman Young to jailed former Mayor Kwame Kilpatrick. When Detroit went bankrupt in 2013, it was the final result of decades of failed policy decisions based on central planning.

When financial analysts look at Eight Mile Road, they see the tragedy of a once-proud city separated. On one side of the road, Detroit; on the other side, Detroit without the mismanagement. To fix the situation would require good governance -- slashing regulations, lowering taxes, attracting business, creating jobs.

Instead, politicians offer more of the same. This week, Attorney General Eric Holder stated that America's racial disparities are a result of continued racism and suggested that neutral laws had reinforced an enduring "subtle racism" throughout the country. Holder cited particular disciplinary practices in schools and sentencing guidelines as repositories of racism.

None of this will heal Detroit or places like it. Economic health requires a dedicated workforce, a free entrepreneurial climate, protection against crime. Those, in turn, require solid two-parent families, a competitive educational environment and a dedication to equal application of the law rather than equal results under it.

Eight Mile Road is a blot on a once-beautiful city. It will remain a dividing line so long as America's politicians continue to use it as one.

Does Obama Care About the Troops?

May 28, 2014

On the day before Memorial Day, President Barack Obama secretly flew into Afghanistan for a surprise visit to the troops. "We're going to stay strong by taking care of our wounded warriors and our veterans. Because helping our wounded warriors and veterans heal isn't just a promise, it's a sacred obligation ... I'm here to say that I'm proud of you," he stated.

But he wasn't in Afghanistan out of mere pride for the troops. As usual, Obama was using the troops for political purposes. Whether he's taking credit for their successful missions ("Today, at my direction, the United States launched a targeted operation against that compound in Abbottabad, Pakistan") or portraying them as victims of brutal, hawkish foreign policy (we "have seen over 3,000 lives of the bravest young Americans wasted" in Iraq), the troops are but implements in Obama's quest for political victory.

And so Obama headed for Afghanistan when news broke that hospitals with the Veterans Affairs had falsified waitlists, resulting in the deaths of dozens of veterans. Because he cares.

This follows a long pattern for Obama. In April 2009, Obama flew to Iraq for a surprise visit. The press dutifully recorded accounts of cheering throngs of troops eager to get a picture of the president with their cameras. They did not, however, report on allegations at the time that soldiers were pre-screened for placement at the Obama event, and that cameras were handed out to the troops.

In October 2009, Obama got up early -- earlier even than he usually does for his tee times -- to visit Dover Air Force Base, Delaware, and watch the coffins of fallen soldiers come home, amid accusations that the war in Afghanistan was spiraling out of control.

The New York Times reported, "The images and the sentiment of the president's five-hour trip to Delaware were intended by the White House to convey to the nation that Mr. Obama was not making his Afghanistan decision lightly or in haste." That sentence disappeared from the original report shortly after it hit the Internet.

The following month, Obama visited Osan Air Base in South Korea, where he stood before troops and stated, "you guys make a pretty good photo op." He used that perspective to its full advantage one month later, when he announced his short-term, midlevel surge in Afghanistan at West Point (New York).

And, of course, when push came to shove during his re-election campaign, Obama showed up -- surprise! -- in Afghanistan, on the one-year anniversary of the killing of Osama bin Laden, where he stated, "The goal that I set -- to defeat al-Qaida and deny it a chance to rebuild -- is now within our reach."

Obama has slashed military funding at historic levels; he insisted that sequestration cuts come largely from the Defense Department. His Veterans Affairs is a shambles, yet he won't fire his top man, Eric Shinseki. Iraq is collapsing. Afghanistan will soon follow.

But he routinely claims that he loves the troops.

Do you believe him?

Barack Obama, Judge of Life or Death

June 4, 2014

On Sept. 30, 2011, two American Predator drones based out of a Saudi Arabian CIA facility swept into Yemen and fired Hellfire missiles at a car containing terrorist and American citizen Anwar al-Awlaki. He was killed. So, too, was terrorist buddy Samir Khan, an American born in Saudi Arabia. President Barack Obama promptly announced the kill: "The death of Awlaki is a major blow to al-Qaida's most active operational affiliate. He took the lead in planning and directing efforts to murder innocent Americans ... and he repeatedly called on individuals in the United States and around the globe to kill innocent men, women and children to advance a murderous agenda." Nowhere did Obama mention that either man was an American citizen.

Last Saturday, Obama announced that the United States had traded five Taliban terrorist leaders in exchange for American Sgt. Bowe Bergdahl. As the days passed, it became clear that Bergdahl was no American hero: he was, in fact, a deserter. He left a note at his base in Afghanistan on June 30, 2009, stating that he hated the military; he emailed his father stating that he hated America. Reports a year later from the U.K. Daily Mail stated that Bergdahl was teaching the Taliban bomb-making and had converted to Islam.

When asked about these problematic issues, Obama immediately signaled that Bergdahl's status as an American was an overriding factor in bartering terrorists for his release. "Whatever those circumstances may turn out to be, we still get an American soldier back if he's held in captivity. Period. Full stop," Obama lectured. Former Secretary of State Hillary Clinton also jumped into the act: "This young man, whatever the circumstances, was an American citizen -- is an American citizen -- was serving in our military. The idea that you really care for your own citizens and particularly those in uniform, I think is a very noble one."

The point here is not that Bergdahl should have been droned, or that al-Awlaki shouldn't have been. The point is that the president of the United States now has the apparent authority to determine whether or not someone deserves to live -- indeed, whether he deserves to be hit with a Hellfire missile or whether we should exchange high-level terrorists for him. And no one can stop the president in such decision-making. He is the judge, jury, and either executioner or savior. He is all-powerful.

This should be frightening to anyone with a modicum of common sense. American citizenship is now, apparently, a malleable commodity. Vice President Joe Biden believes that illegal immigrants are citizens. Obama believes that some Americans who join Islamist groups are citizens, while others are not. Who is an American? Whomever the executive branch deems an American. Who isn't? It depends on whether Obama ate his Wheaties or not.

Either American citizenship counts for something, or it does not. Either joining America's enemies strips you of your rights, or it does not. But when the president of the United States can arbitrarily decide whether or not those rights have been stripped, all of our rights have been stripped.

Prosecute the President

June 11, 2014

President Barack Obama believes he is above the law.

That's because he is.

This week alone, Obama announced that he would unilaterally change student loan rules, allowing borrowers to avoid paying off more of their debt; he signaled that he would continue his non-enforcement of immigration law, even as thousands of children cross the border; he defended his non-disclosure of a terrorist swap to Congress.

And, he said, more such actions were in the offing. "I will keep doing whatever I can without Congress," Obama explained.

This is not just executive overreach. In many cases, Obama's exercise of authoritarian power is criminal. His executive branch is responsible for violations of the Arms Export Control Act in shipping weapons to Syria, the Espionage Act in Libya, and IRS law with regard to the targeting of conservative groups. His executive branch is guilty of involuntary manslaughter in Benghazi and in the Fast and Furious scandal, and bribery in its allocation of waivers in Obamacare and tax dollars in its stimulus spending. His administration is guilty of obstruction of justice and witness tampering.

And yet nothing is done.

Impeachment, which has been suggested as a solution by many, is a non-starter. In the entire history of the republic, the House has impeached just 19 officials, and just eight were actually removed from office after Senate trial. Impeachment is a political solution to a criminal problem -- and politicians are far too fearful of blowback to use it as a tool in upholding law.

Thanks to presidential immunity and executive control of the Justice Department, there are no consequences to executive branch lawbreaking. And when it comes to presidential lawbreaking, the sitting president could literally strangle someone to death on national television and meet with no consequences. As Professor Akhil Reed Amar of Yale Law School has written, "a sitting President is constitutionally immune from ordinary criminal prosecution -- state or federal."

So what can we do? We can tell Congress to delegate its power to check the executive branch. The Racketeer Influenced and Corrupt Organizations Act creates a broad capacity for prosecution of criminal conspiracies; it also provides for civil lawsuits against such conspiracies, turning American citizens into, as the Supreme Court puts it, "'private attorneys general' on a serious national problem for which public prosecutorial resources are deemed inadequate." Minor changes to the law should allow citizens to sue federal officials within the executive branch under RICO, unmasking criminal enterprises within the Obama administration and future administrations.

The checks and balances of the Constitution have failed. The result has been, for a century, the nearly unchecked growth of the power of the executive branch. That growth has created an executive tyranny, unanswerable and inescapable under law. Our legislators have proved themselves too cowardly to fight back using the tools at their disposal. They are obviously happy delegating their power to the executive branch. Now it's time for them to delegate their power to the people.

How Fatherhood Made Me a Better Person

June 18, 2014

My baby daughter has ruined me.

I'm not typically known for being the most openly emotional person. On the incredibly rare occasions in which I find myself crying -- typically when the last track of "The Many Adventures of Winnie the Pooh" pipes through the car stereo (why would you leave the Hundred Acre Wood, Christopher Robin, you dolt?!) -- my wife revels in it. The first time it happened, she turned to me, grinning gleefully, and exclaimed, "You do have feelings!"

At least, that's how it was until Leeya was born.

Now I'm a wreck.

Last week, my 4-month-old began crying when we put her down to sleep at night. I put my hand on her chest and began rocking her back and forth. Her crying gradually reduced to cooing, and then finally she dozed off.

Maybe she wasn't crying anymore, but I was. I found myself tearing up because I couldn't help but think of a time, decades from now, when she's in pain, and I won't be there to help. I won't be there to rock her to sleep or to put her head on my shoulder or to tell her everything will be all right.

Every so often, we all gaze into the abyss. It's a depressing fact of life that eventually the clock expires, eventually the sand in the hourglass runs out. It's the leaving behind of everything that matters to us that hurts the most.

Which is why what we do now matters.

In his weekly Internet address, President Barack Obama tackled Father's Day by repeating a line from his 2013 State of the Union address: "what makes you a man isn't the ability to have a child -- it's the courage to raise one." But, of course, it doesn't take courage to raise your child; it takes common decency. Only reprobates father children and then abandon them.

What really makes you man, I've realized, is not merely providing for and defending your wife, or even raising your child -- it's the action that lies in the realization that the future matters, even if you won't be here to see it. In an era in which immediate gratification and self-discovery are now given moral priority over delayed gratification and moral action, our children show us the barrenness of such a view. The words of Beyonce and Pepsi at the Super Bowl -- "Live for now!" -- ring false when you look at your crying child and understand that decades hence, your life won't have mattered a damn if you didn't live it for her.

Having children truly ends adolescence. We are all either parents or children: responsibility-takers or those who demand from others. Which is why it's such a human tragedy that Western civilization has now prized endless childhood as the ultimate ideal. When the president of the United States characterizes fatherhood as some sort of act of bravery, but the capacity to murder the unborn as a human right, society itself comes unmoored.

But we can anchor it again. Every time we rock our babies in the night, we bring order back to a disordered world. Every time we look down at our children and cry, we make the world one shade brighter. That's what children do to us -- and for us. That's what Leeya has done for me.

Welcome to the Executive Dictatorship

June 25, 2014

The Constitution is dead.

Long live the executive dictatorship.

There is almost nothing the president of the United States cannot do. This week, we found out President Barack Obama's IRS not only targeted conservative nonprofit applicants with impunity but then destroyed the emails that could have illuminated the process behind such targeting. Meanwhile, the attorney general -- the executive officer charged with fighting government criminality -- continues to stonewall an independent prosecutor, maintaining along with his boss that there is not a "smidgen of corruption" in the IRS.

On the southern border, Immigration and Customs Enforcement has been converted from a policing agency to a humanitarian-aid agency, as the Obama administration encourages thousands of unaccompanied minors to flood Texas and Arizona. Those illegal immigrants are being shuttled around the southwest and released into the general population, and told by activists that they are just months away from amnesty.

Across the seas, Obama is unilaterally destroying America's anti-terror infrastructure. Iraq has become the preserve of the al-Qaida offshoot ISIS and the Iranian-connected Shiite government -- the specific outcome the United States originally wanted to avoid in the country. Afghanistan will soon devolve back into a Taliban-led cesspool for terror. And the Obama administration continues to fund a Palestinian government that includes terrorist groups Hamas and Islamic Jihad, and that has now kidnapped an American citizen, along with two other Israeli boys.

Nobody in the executive branch has been punished for Benghazi, Libya, Fast and Furious, serious national security leaks to major news outlets, violations of civil rights by the National Security Agency or any other major scandal. The Obama administration has seized authority to regulate health care, carbon emissions and labor relations in unforeseen ways.

And no one will stop the executive branch. Impeachment will not solve the problem of a 3 million-strong regulatory branch in which accountability is a fantasy. The legislature has no interest in stopping the growth of the executive, given that legislators seek re-election by avoiding responsibility, and granting more power to the executive avoids such responsibility. And the judiciary seems unwilling to hem in the executive branch at all, given its decisions on the Environmental Protection Agency and Obamacare.

So what's left? An elected tyranny in which the whims of the president and all of his men decide the fate of millions. The founders would have fought such a government with every fiber of their being -- and, in fact, they did fight such a government. The question now is whether state governments, elected officials and the people themselves will be willing to take the measures necessary to do the same.

The Jew-Hating Obama Administration

July 2, 2014

On Monday, three Jewish boys were found dead, murdered by the terrorist group Hamas: Eyal Yifrach, 19; Gilad Shaar, 16; and Naftali Frenkel, 16. Frenkel was an American citizen. The three were kidnapped while hitchhiking some three weeks ago. In the interim, President Barack Obama said nothing about them publicly. His wife issued no hashtags. His State Department maintained that $400 million in American taxpayer cash would continue to the Palestinian unity government, which includes Hamas.

Presumably Frenkel did not look enough like Barack Obama's imaginary son for him to give a damn. Or perhaps Frenkel hadn't deserted his duty in the American military, and therefore his parents didn't deserve a White House press conference. Maybe Michelle Obama was too busy worrying about children's fat thighs to spend a moment tweeting out a selfie to raise awareness.

Or maybe, just maybe, the Obama administration didn't care about Frenkel because he was a Jew.

Jewish blood is cheap to this administration. That seems to be true in every administration, given the American government's stated predilection for forcing Israel into concessions to an implacable and Jew-hating enemy. But it's particularly true for an administration that has now cut a deal with Iran that legitimizes its government, weakens sanctions, and forestalls Israeli action against its nuclear program. It's especially true for an administration that forced the Israeli government to apologize to the Turkish government for stopping a terrorist flotilla aimed at supplying Hamas. And it's undoubtedly true for an administration that has undercut Israeli security at every turn, deposing Hosni Mubarak in

Egypt, fostering chaos in Syria and by extension destabilizing Jordan and Lebanon, and leaking Israeli national security information no less than four times.

Now the corpse of a 16-year-old Jewish American is found in Hebron.

The Obama administration's first response: to call on the Israeli government for restraint. State Department spokeswoman Jen Psaki said on June 2, "Based on what we know now, we intend to work with this government." Now, just a month later, that government has murdered an American kid. And now she says that the Obama administration hopes "that the Israelis and the Palestinians continue to work with one another on that, and we certainly would continue to urge that ... in spite of, obviously, the tragedy and the enormous pain on the ground."

To which the proper Israeli response should be: go perform anatomically impossible acts upon yourself.

The Obama administration had the opportunity to stand clearly against Jew-hating evil. Not only did it fail to do so but it funded that evil, encouraged that evil, militated against fighting that evil. But that's nothing new. Jew hatred is as old as the Jewish people. It's just found a new home in the White House.

Never Let a Self-Produced Horror Show Go to Waste

July 9, 2014

"You never want a serious crisis to go to waste," President Barack Obama's former chief of staff, Rahm Emanuel, once infamously stated. He never bothered to spell out the unspoken corollary to that appalling statement: And if there is no serious crisis available, manufacture one.

The American left has followed that pattern for generations. The left destroyed the nuclear family by incentivizing women to give birth out of wedlock. When out-of-wedlock births exploded, they used that as an excuse to elevate federal spending, elevate taxes and disestablish marriage between a man and a woman as a moral standard. The left crafted a health care crisis by instituting price and wage controls that led to employer-sponsored insurance, and then undercut that insurance with excessive regulation and easy lawsuits. They used elevating costs as an excuse to push Obamacare and elevate taxes.

Now, the left, under Obama, has crafted the mother of all crises: an influx of tens of thousands of unaccompanied minors crossing America's southern border. Some of these minors carry disease. Virtually all carry wounds, either physical or psychological, from their criminal coyote guides. That crisis is not Obama's Hurricane Katrina, as some have speculated. Katrina was an act of God, and its botched handling the act of men. This entire situation is an act of Obama. And he couldn't be happier as he watches frustrated Americans take to the streets in Murrieta, California, to protest his lawlessness.

Obama created this situation, and he certainly knows how to exploit it. Obama wants to campaign based on the suffering of these children. He wants to push for higher taxes based on their unequal economic status. He wants their eventual votes for the left. He wants the federal government to punish American citizens tired of watching their government abandon them.

It's all part of the agenda.

Obama and the media maintain the absurd fiction that Obama was thunderstruck by this crisis. Obama himself has assured the public that he wants all of the new arrivals sent home forthwith and that they were foolish to believe they could stay.

Foolish?

Four years ago, the Obama Justice Department sued the state of Arizona for daring to enforce federal immigration law, and sanctuary cities across the country remained unscathed. Two years ago, Obama declared that all illegal immigrants between the ages of 16 and 30 who had not committed criminal felonies -- the so-called Dreamers -- would remain in the country. This week, the Ninth Circuit Court of Appeals ruled that Arizona would have to hand out driver's licenses to the Dreamers, and the city of Los Angeles announced it would no longer cooperate with Immigration and Customs Enforcement in holding requested illegals for 48 hours after their jail terms expired.

Those desperate to come to America would be fools not to jump at the chance. And their dangerous decisions to send their own children across thousands of miles of desert in the company of likely drug cartel associates underscores their certainty: They're willing to risk the lives of their children, knowing that so long as the children get to the border, Obama will legitimize them, and then, by extension, their entire families.

This, of course, is precisely what Obama wanted them to think. Now he has his crisis. And he'll exploit it for everything it's worth, no matter how much blood is spilled in the deserts of Mexico or the streets of Murrieta.

Bloodguilt Over Jews Leads to Blood Libels Against Jews

July 16, 2014

If there's one place on Earth that should understand the danger of Jew hatred, it is Frankfurt, Germany. In 1933, boycotts targeted Jews; by 1938, Germans were burning synagogues down. Between 1933 and 1945, the Jewish population of the city was decimated, dropping from 30,000 to 602. Few Jews, most of them Soviet expatriates, live in the city now.

So Frankfurt seems an odd place for a new blood libel against the Jews. Nonetheless, this week, 2,500 protesters, including Muslims and neo-Nazis -- allied once again -- showed up downtown to scream about Israel's defensive action against Hamas in the Gaza Strip. Police reportedly helped out the protesters, allowing them to utilize a loudspeaker and a vehicle to shout anti-Israel diatribes. "You Jews Are Beasts," read one sign.

Meanwhile, in Paris, Muslims attacked two Jewish synagogues, including one in which 150 Jews had gathered to mourn the deaths of three Jewish boys, who were murdered by Hamas operatives. Those Muslims, brandishing bats and chairs, attempted to break into the synagogue and ended up injuring several Jews. In recent years, thousands of Jews from France have emigrated to Israel, amid shocking reports of beatings, stabbings and an ax attack.

The Europeans, it seems, are becoming increasingly comfortable with old-fashioned Jew hatred in their midst, whether homegrown or imported.

There's a reason for that. In much of Europe, bloodguilt over the Holocaust still hangs over the heads of the population. According to a 2012 Anti-Defamation League survey of European countries, 45 percent of Austrians, 35 percent of French, 43 percent of Germans, 63 percent of Hungarians and 53 percent of Polish citizens felt that it was "probably true" that "Jews still talk too much about what happened to them in the Holocaust." Many of those who wish to move beyond the Holocaust, therefore, look for a rationale to relieve national guilt -- and what better way to relieve national guilt than to label the Jewish State an aggressor? After all, if the Jews have become the villains, then why spend too much time thinking about their victimization?

Of course, the labeling of Jews as bloodthirsty villains led to the Holocaust in the first place. Adolf Hitler saw the Jews as bloodsuckers driven by greed and dual loyalty. So did much of the rest of Europe. In the minds of those who murdered Jews en masse, Jews had it coming, because, in the words of Hitler: "The struggle for world domination will be fought entirely between us -- between Germans and Jews. All else is facade and illusion."

Those who today label Israel the font of all evil use Hitler's rationale to relieve guilt over Hitler. That's why the same protesters in Frankfurt threatening Jews carried posters comparing Israel to the Nazis: If Jews are the new Nazis, fighting the Jews becomes an obligation.

Every Passover, Jews recite a paragraph: "in every generation they rise against us to destroy us; and the Holy One, blessed be He, saves us from their hand!" The names change, but the rationale does not. And the God of Israel is always watching, even if those who attack the Jews have convinced themselves that He will turn a blind eye.

Why Vladimir Putin Is Kicking Barack Obama's Behind

July 23, 2014

On Monday, four days after Vladimir Putin's minions in Ukraine shot down a passenger airliner carrying 298 people, including an American citizen, President Barack Obama emerged from the White House to issue a statement. Scowling at the camera, Obama stated: "Russia has extraordinary influence over these separatists. No one denies that. Russia has urged them on. Russia has trained them."

Finally, after fulminating for several minutes about the nastiness of the Russian government, Obama approached the predictable climax: threats of action.

Except that there were none.

Instead, Obama explained that if Russia were to ignore his warnings, it would "only further isolate itself from the international community, and the costs for Russia's behavior will only continue to increase."

To which Putin's only rational response would be laughter.

This is a Western humiliation on an epic scale. Obama and Europe could wrongly and weakly pass off the invasion and annexation of Crimea as a historical anomaly brutally corrected. They could ignore the further invasion of eastern Ukraine, focusing instead on those naughty Israelis busily defending themselves against rocket attacks from Hamas terrorists.

But now, the West has told Putin, in no uncertain terms, that his people can hit a civilian aircraft with a missile, and that there will be no costs.

How can a second-rate power hold the United States and NATO over a barrel?

Vice President Joe Biden gave the answer in an interview with The New Yorker, albeit unwittingly (though that should go without saying, given Biden's witlessness). While bragging about his gung-ho, macho political attitude, Biden related a story about meeting Putin -- a story he pledged was "absolutely, positively" true, meaning there is a three in four chance it is complete fiction.

But, taking the vice president at his word, the story went like this. Biden met Putin at the Kremlin in 2011. They found themselves standing face to face. "I said, 'Mr. Prime Minister, I'm looking into your eyes, and I don't think you have a soul,'" Biden related to interviewer. "And he looked back at me, and he smiled, and he said, 'We understand one another.' This is who this guy is."

The last line from Biden is the key to the story: He sees Putin's response as a defeat for Putin somehow, a denial of his humanity. Putin, Biden seems to be saying, is an inhuman James Bond villain -- and for some reason, Biden thinks this widespread perception of Putin makes him weak.

But that's Putin's entire goal : He wants the West to believe he has no soul. While the West, like Biden, seeks to demonstrate its bigheartedness to Putin, with "reset" buttons and U.N. resolutions and G8 summits and Olympic Games, Putin seeks to demonstrate that he has no heart. He wants to be seen as cruel and inhuman. He wants everyone to know that he will never bluff and that he will always shoot first.

Obama, Biden and the European Union somehow believe that handwringing and moral proclamations will bring Putin into line. Putin knows strength -- or, at least, the impression of intransigent steeliness -- will bring the West into line. In a game of chicken, the man who openly puts a brick on the accelerator will always win.

Putin's got the brick on the accelerator. He's had quite a hot streak: Georgia, Syria, Iran and now Ukraine. The result will be a far more dangerous world, as potential Russian targets seek nuclear weapons to deter the bear, and as Putin speeds to consolidate his gains. Obama's nuclear-free world, his multipolar United Nations geopolitics, spirals the toilet, thanks to his own utopian wishful thinking.

This is what happens when children play against adults on the world stage. This is what happens when starry-eyed post-Americans are given charge of Western leadership. Putin rolls on, evilly manipulating, grossly murdering. And Obama makes peeved faces as bodies smolder in Ukrainian fields.

Obama: Troll Hard With a Vengeance

July 30, 2014

This week, as I have been predicting for months, President Barack Obama announced that he would be considering unprecedented executive action to provide legal status for millions of illegal immigrants. His goal is not to solve the immigration crisis -- you don't grant legal status to 5 million illegal immigrants, then leave the back door wide open if you're interested in solving the problem. His goal is not to help illegal immigrants -- he instead leaves them in limbo by granting them temporary work permits, rather than blanket amnesty.

His goal is trolling.

Trolling is a practice whereby a person takes a deliberately indefensible position simply to draw passionate excess from an opponent. That is Obama's goal here: He hopes for extreme language, impassioned opposition and eventually, impeachment.

This administration is hungry for impeachment. While no Republican leader in Congress has given even a smidgen of credibility to impeachment talk, the Obama administration has been fundraising off impeachment rumors. Last Friday, the White House said that it was not dismissing the possibility of a House impeachment; senior adviser Dan Pfeiffer said that Obama "would not discount the possibility." Two weeks ago, Obama brought up the possibility of impeachment in order to mock it to his supporters. As Politico noted, "Who's talking about impeachment? Barack Obama."

Joe Trippi, a Democratic consultant, explained why Democrats love impeachment talk: "The more they talk about it, the more it has a red hot effect on their base. So if you can get the temperature just right, you're turning out all your base voters, and Democrats don't take it seriously, and it's a good year for you. If that stove gets just a little too hot, and you lose control of it, you're going to have every Democrat on the planet turning out to stop it."

Obama trolls because he recognizes that trends cut against Democrats in 2014. If he believed that Democrats were well-positioned to win back the House of Representatives, he would threaten executive action and then call on Americans to give his party a majority. Instead, he seeks to gin up outrage on the right and enthusiasm on the left. And he'll use the lives of millions of Americans and non-Americans to do it. It's a desperation play, but it's his only play.

That's because Obama has no capacity for compromise. His strategy has always been simple: govern when you have a majority; campaign when you don't. And so, for the last several years, he's spent significantly more time doing fundraisers than being president -- and even when he's being president, he's simply setting up the next stop in his endless campaign.

So what should conservatives do? First off, they should stop talking impeachment. It's a waste of time and effort. It serves no purpose. It is not principled to talk impeachment; it is idiotic. There are zero Democrats in the Senate who would vote to convict Obama and few Republicans.

Second, conservatives should point out that Obama does not have the country's best interests in mind. He does not care about the fate of illegal immigrants -- if he did, he'd stop incentivizing children to travel thousands of miles in the hands of coyotes, then offering uncertainty as to their status, incentivizing thousands more to do the same. He obviously does not care about the political climate of the country -- if he did, he'd stop manipulating and start governing.

Finally, conservatives should ignore Obama. His rhetoric is unimportant. It is a distraction. They should focus instead on his actions, which are deliberately designed to undermine the country for his own political gain.

How the Media Craft Victory for Hamas

August 6, 2014

On Tuesday, CNN's Wolf Blitzer hosted Hamas spokesman Osama Hamden. The week before, Hamdan labeled Israeli Prime Minister Benjamin Netanyahu "a new image of Hitler" on the network. But now, for some reason, Blitzer stumbled into a random act of journalism: He asked Hamdan about comments he had made suggesting that Jews used Christian blood in matza. Hamdan stumbled around and blamed the Jews for their action in Gaza.

Blitzer called Hamdan's comments an "awful, awful smear."

The very fact that this represented a unique moment in the media coverage of the Israel-Hamas Gaza war demonstrates the malpractice of the media. The first questions on the media's collective tongue should have been: What does Hamas stand for? What are its goals? Why does it use women and children as human shields? Why does it hide military resources in civilian areas?

But that had to wait for a month.

In the meantime, CNN viewers saw an unending stream of dramatic images from Gaza of Palestinian Arab suffering: heavy blasts from Israeli ordinance, screaming women, bleeding children. Every so often, CNN punctuated its coverage with death toll statistics -- never mentioning that it received those statistics from the Palestinians themselves, and neglecting to mention the Palestinians' regular practice of classifying dead terrorists as civilians. Then CNN asked questions about Israeli "proportionality" and wondered aloud about whether Israeli strikes were sufficiently "targeted."

If you want to know why the conflict between the dramatically overpowering Israeli military and the sadistically brutal Hamas has continued for weeks, look no further than CNN and its like-minded media brethren. Hamas' goals in this conflict did not include military victory; Hamas may be evil, but it is not stupid. Its main goal was to shore up its base by achieving small concessions from Israel and Egypt, as well as the Palestinian Authority; those concessions could only be achieved if Israel could be portrayed as an international aggressor against a terror group.

And that's where the media manipulation came in. Hamas placed heavy restrictions on journalists and even threatened them. Hamas put women and children and mentally ill people in harm's way for the cameras, and as a deterrent to Israeli military action.

And the media went right along with it, proclaiming balance all the way. When I was on CNN this week with Alisyn Camerota, she maintained that CNN provided balance by presenting "both sides," to which I responded that presenting both sides in a battle between Hamas and Israel is not balance, but anti-Israel bias. No Western media member would, in 1944, have assumed that balance meant quoting both Winston Churchill and Julius Streicher. To do so would have been to forward propaganda.

But that is precisely what the media have done. They have turned balance into a synonym for amorality. In doing so, they have handed a propaganda victory to evil.

Let's Get Serious About Mental Illness

August 13, 2014

Robin Williams' suicide this week shook up people across the political spectrum -- and for good reason. When a highly successful, incredibly popular figure from our culture decides to take his own life, it feels as though suicide could happen to anyone.

It can't.

Robin Williams reportedly suffered from mentally illness. He stated during an interview in 2006 that he hadn't been formally diagnosed with depression or bipolar disorder, but stated, "Do I perform sometimes in a manic style? Yes. Am I manic all the time? No. Do I get sad? Oh yeah. Does it hit me hard? Oh yeah." He added, "I get bummed, like I think a lot of us do at certain times. You look at the world and go, 'Whoa.' Other moments you look and go, 'Oh, things are OK.'" That same year, according to the Huffington Post, he explained the temptation of alcoholism -- he had famously admitted to drug and alcohol addiction problems -- to Diane Sawyer. "It's the same voice thought that ... you're standing at a precipice and you look down, there's a voice and it's a little quiet voice that goes, 'Jump.'"

Williams' death has spurred multiple writers and celebrities to announce their own struggles with such issues; virtually every family has suffered through the horrors of mental illness. My grandfather was diagnosed with bipolar disorder decades ago, and routinely battled suicidality until his introduction to lithium.

Raising awareness is praiseworthy - the stigma attached to getting help for mental illness should be wiped away as soon as possible.

By the same token, we ought to ensure that normalizing mental illness helps no one, and damages those who truly are mentally ill. The lack of awareness surrounding mental illness comes from two directions: first, those who pretend that mental illness represents a lack of willpower or dedication; second, those who pretend that serious mental illnesses are not mental illnesses at all, but representations of free thought and behavior. Forty years ago, the first group predominated; today, the second does.

Forty years ago, men and women feared career destruction should rumors spread that they were seeing psychologists or psychiatrists. That fear has largely dissipated. But a new threat to the well-being of those suffering from mental illness has replaced the original threat: the threat of diversity campaigners leaving those with mental illness to suffer in the name of heterogeneity.

This is not to suggest that all of those who are "different" are mentally ill, or vice versa. But it is meant to suggest that we ought to consider the mental health of those who are homeless, rather than labeling them, in blanket fashion, advocates for free living spaces. It is meant to suggest that those who suffer from gender dysphoria may not be suffering from societal bigotry, but from something far deeper and more dangerous, and that physical mutilation and stumping for tolerance will not solve their problems.

In other words, if we are to recognize the importance of mental illness as a society, the left must stop papering over mental illness with platitudes about diversity, and the right must stop treating mental illness as a moral problem rather than a medical one. Those racked with mental anguish are crying out for our help. If we don't hear them, it may be because too busy pushing political viewpoints rather than listening.

The Great Racial Disconnect on Police

August 20, 2014

On Monday, Rasmussen released a poll of Americans regarding the guilt or innocence of Officer Darren Wilson, the police officer who shot unarmed 18-year-old black man Michael Brown six times in Ferguson, Missouri. Those polls show that 57 percent of black adults think that Wilson should be found guilty of murder; 56 percent of whites, by contrast, are undecided on the matter.

The latter position is the correct one. Witnesses, including one Dorian Johnson, claim that Brown was pulled over by Wilson, attacked by him and pulled into the car, ran, stopped when told to freeze by Wilson, held up his hands, and was then shot. Other witnesses -- more than a dozen of them, according to local media -- say that Brown attacked Wilson, went for Wilson's gun, fled before being told to stop, then charged Wilson before being shot.

Here's what we do know: Despite original media reports labeling Brown a "gentle giant," Brown and shooting witness Dorian Johnson did participate in a strong-arm robbery of a local convenience store. We know that despite original witness reports suggesting that Brown was shot in the back, he was not. We know that contemporaneous witness accounts caught on tape suggest that Brown charged at Wilson. And we know that a young black man is dead with six bullets in him at the hands of a white cop.

And to huge segments of the black community, that last fact is the only one that matters. The full facts do not matter to extremists in the black community and to their white leftist enablers, particularly in the media. A full 41 percent of black Americans believe that riots and looting represent "legitimate outrage." Not protesting -- riots and looting. Just 35 percent of blacks think that looters and rioters are criminals taking advantage of the situation.

There is a pattern here: a widespread belief in the black community that the justice system is rigged against them. That belief is not without basis -- there is no question that America has a history of racism within the criminal justice community. By the same token, there is also no question that American law enforcement is the least racist it has ever been, by a long shot, and that racism within the law enforcement community is broadly considered unacceptable and vile.

But the belief in a racist justice system seems to have maintained its stranglehold inside the black community. That belief, taken to its extreme, means support for black criminality. It is no coincidence that during the O.J. Simpson trial, 60 percent of black Americans did not believe O.J. was guilty. It is also no coincidence that many white Americans perceive black support for murderers like O.J. Simpson and riots in Ferguson as support for lawlessness, and therefore pooh-pooh charges of police racism. When crying racism becomes crying wolf, it is hard to take such charges seriously.

The solution, however, lays neither in knee-jerk accusations of racism from the black community nor in immediate dismissals of individual accusations by the white community. It lies in continued targeting and prosecution of individual racists in the police community, of course -- and far more importantly, it lies in less criminality within the black community. The high levels of crime in the black community contribute to heavier policing, which in turn reinforces perceptions of racial targeting; those perceptions then create resentment against police than ends too often in violent encounters and failure to report crime. And so the cycle starts anew.

It's time to break the cycle. The only way to do that is to focus on the fact that police have no excuse to shoot anyone unless those people are committing criminal acts. On that we can all agree. Yes, we must arduously insist that police hold to that standard, and we must prosecute those who do not to the fullest extent of the law. But by the same token, we must insist that criminal acts stop -- and to do that, we must move beyond simple anti-police sentiment.

Those Who Go Unsung

August 27, 2014

The vast majority of Americans have never met Phil Weinberg.

But that isn't because he's unimportant. It's because he is important. Like millions of Americans who toil largely in anonymity, participating daily in acts of courage and generosity, Phil has never been on CNN or Fox News; while he subscribes to The Wall Street Journal, he's never had his picture dot pixelated. That's because he, like so many other Americans, is too busy making the country work.

Phil was born at the Beth Israel Hospital in Boston in 1951, just down the block from Fenway Park, and grew up a diehard Red Sox fan (of course). He began working as a kid, selling papers on a street corner for eight cents a pop, shoveling snow for neighbors. He headed his junior congregation while still a kid at Hebrew school -- where his future wife, Cheryl, saw him, although she had no clue she'd end up marrying the tall, goofy guy who was leading services.

Phil knew early on he wanted to be a teacher. He majored in education at Boston University, got another bachelor's in Jewish education simultaneously at Hebrew University, and then studied Jewish history at Jewish Theological Seminary. He worked his way through college on work study as a janitor, flipped burgers and sold Drake's cakes to other starving students. Phil actually met his wife, Cheryl, when they were both students at Hebrew College. They were best friend for six years. Then they realized what they had, and decided to get married. Their life was just beginning.

Phil and Cheryl moved down to Tampa, Florida, where Phil taught at a Hebrew day school. His teaching career took him back to Boston, then to El Paso, Texas, and finally to California -- he earned two more master's degrees in Texas and California. That's where he got out of Jewish education and into general education at the Los Angeles Unified School District. One of the roughest school districts in the country, LAUSD is perennially underperforming; its student population includes some of the most poverty-stricken areas in the United States.

Phil jumped in with both feet. He taught special education, a self-contained class for children with specific learning disabilities -- but since LAUSD was badly administered, the district threw all sorts of children in Phil's classes, including autistic kids, developmental delays and emotionally disturbed children.

Despite the challenges of LAUSD's administrative chaos, Phil sought to teach these kids, many of whom had parents who either couldn't or wouldn't raise their children. He taught the children, many of whom were immigrants to the country, patriotic songs, even though the district disapproved of such political incorrectness. He read them stories, making sure to play all the parts. He created specific goals and reports for each student.

These kids were his kids.

Phil and Cheryl were never able to conceive naturally, so they adopted a son. Their son was troubled, but they poured their heart and soul into raising him, just as they pour themselves into everything they did.

Phil is my uncle -- not the brother of my mom or dad, but an adopted uncle. He is best friends with my father. And my father only has one rule for his friends: They must treat his children with kindness and generosity. Phil is the epitome of both.

My father always said as we were growing up that surrounding your children with good people is one of the chief tasks of a parent. My parents certainly did that with Phil. He is an intellectual, a brilliant man, well-read, soft-spoken. He always provides information, but he is never strident, never arrogant. He is a friend, an advisor, and a mentor. And he is never happier than when I or my sisters tell him about what we're achieving and what battles we're fighting.

I'm writing about Phil now because he's in a hospital in California. He's been battling cancer for several years; last week, he had a stroke. He's still fighting, and he'll still keep fighting. Because that's what we do as Americans. We may never get our 15 minutes of fame. We may never get our headshot on cable television. But we will make the country work, teach the next generation, and do so because we are a generous and forgiving people, willing to slog in the trenches without fame or fortune.

That's my uncle Phil.

Of Racial Delusions and Riots

September 3, 2014

Last week, as riots in Ferguson, Missouri decrescendoed and the country held its collective breath over the question of the indictment of Officer Darren Wilson in the shooting death of Michael Brown, rappers Diddy (formerly P. Diddy, formerly Puff Daddy, formerly Sean Combs), 2 Chainz, The Game, and Rick Ross, along with 10 of their fellows, released a song: "Don't Shoot."

The Game explained why he felt the necessity to record the song: "I am a black man with kids of my own that I love more than anything, and I cannot fathom a horrific tragedy like Michael Brown's happening to them. This possibility has shaken me to my core."

The lyrics of the song speak to a perverse view of race in America -- a view reinforced day after day by a media dedicated to the proposition that American law enforcement maliciously targets black men at random. To this point, nobody knows the facts of the case in the Brown shooting. Nonetheless, the rappers label the shooting cold-blooded, first-degree murder. Because facts are unnecessary; only feelings are real. "God ain't put us on the Earth to get murdered, it's murder," says one rapper, TGT. Another, The Game, raps, "They killin' teens, they killin' dreams, it's murder."

Next, Diddy launches into a listing of various black men killed under controversial circumstances. Some, like Emmett Till, were murdered in acts of pure and evil racism. But Diddy lumps together Till with Trayvon Martin and Michael Brown -- and even Ezell Ford. Last week, the Los Angeles Police Department released the identities of the two police officers who shot Ford. One was Asian; the other was Hispanic. The Huffington Post did not even cover their races.

The Los Angeles Times buried that relevant fact in paragraph 13 of their comprehensive story. But again, facts do not matter: Only a feeling of persecution matters.

Then Rick Ross sums up the generalized view of America created by media-stoked racial conflagrations like the Michael Brown situation: "Black men, we pay the toll, the price is your life, Uncle Sam want a slice, black dress code now we looting in the night, now we throwing Molotovs in this Holocaust." A grand total of just under 100 young black men are killed by white police officers each year, according to statistics provided to the FBI by local police. To compare police treatment of young black men to the Holocaust is not only statistically idiotic, but also morally dangerous.

Nonetheless, that is the view of police for many blacks: police as paramilitary white force out to target black men. When I was recently in the CNN green room with former Obama green jobs czar Van Jones, he and I got to talking about the Ferguson situation. I asked him why he believed there was such a racial gap in the interpretation of the situation. His answer: "You're Jewish, right? Wouldn't you jump to conclusions if you heard that the Nazis or Hamas had killed a Jew?"

Of course, not even Van Jones, Diddy, 2 Chainz, and the rest truly believe what they say about the police. All those who spout about a "Holocaust" by police against blacks would call 911 in approximately 3.5 seconds if their houses were robbed. But if we truly believe that America's police forces are akin to Nazis or Islamic terrorists, there can be no decent solution. Fighting police would be a moral imperative, not a moral evil.

And therein lies the problem. The only real answer to the antipathy between large segments of the black community and police is threefold: first, taking seriously fact-based allegations of racism against the authorities, and investigating and prosecuting such allegations if well-founded; second, not jumping to conclusions about non-fact-based allegations; and third, lowering crime rates among young black men, thereby lowering interactions between police and young black men.

But those are not solutions backed by the racially delusional. Instead, they suggest an unending and circular "conversation" about race that goes something like this: Police sometimes shoot young black men; that's because police are racist; therefore, those who resist police are not morally unjustified; rinse, wash, repeat.

Sadly, America's media backs this second approach. And so we end up with damaging foolishness like "Don't Shoot" infusing our pop culture and the snarky but empty-headed racial guilting of Jon Stewart and Stephen Colbert invading our news. And nothing gets solved. We just get more hate, more rage and more violence.

The Global Map, 2017

September 10, 2014

Barack Obama pledged to radically transform America when he took office. He didn't stop at America. President Obama's greatest legacy may be the radical reshaping of the global map.

Fast forward three years. Here's where we stand.

Given Europe's failure to stand up to Russian aggression in Crimea, Russia's borders have expanded to include Eastern Ukraine, northern Kazakhstan and larger portions of Moldova. As of 2014, Russia had consolidated its hold on Transnistria, the Eastern region of Moldova, which is heavily Russian; Russia had annexed Crimea; Russia had placed troops inside Eastern Ukraine.

But it didn't stop there. Russia began squeezing Georgia again, and pro-Russian regimes are consolidating their power in Kazakhstan and Belarus. Belarus asked the Russian government to place 15 warplanes inside the country in 2014; Kazakhstan got into a tiff with Russia over comments Putin made unsubtly suggesting a possible invasion of the country, then complied with Putin's demands when the West did nothing.

Thus far, Putin has not invaded any NATO countries. But that could change, given the high Russian population in Latvia and Estonia.

Meanwhile, in the Middle East, Jordan's kingdom has fallen, replaced by a radical Islamist regime. That Palestinian Arab regime has attempted to consolidate its power by forming an alliance with Hamas in Judea, Samaria, and Gaza. In Lebanon, the Iranians and Syrians have effectively annexed southern Lebanon. Israel's only quiet border is now its southern border with Egypt.

In Syria, Bashar Assad has retained a measure of power by essentially conceding territory to ISIS in the eastern part of the country; after a halfhearted intervention against ISIS, the international community went quiet as ISIS formed its sought-after caliphate in eastern Syria and northern Iraq. In response, Iran essentially invaded southern Iraq, and Turkey launched covert action against the Kurds in order to prevent the formation of a broader Kurdistan encompassing parts of Turkish territory.

With the withdrawal of the United States and its allies from Afghanistan, Pakistan has once again made its presence felt. The Taliban have effectively taken control of large swaths of territory, with the help of the Pakistani regime, which has shifted leadership but not position with regard to radical Islam.

In the most stunning international move, China has threatened full-scale annexation of Taiwan, barring access to the South China Sea from Western countries and cutting off Taiwan's trade routes. The West has refused to leverage China, fearing financial retaliation. China has made similar moves against the Philippines.

Come 2017, this will be President Obama's legacy: a world of redrawn borders, all to the benefit of some of the worst regimes on the planet. When America retreats from the world, its enemies expand.

The Conversation We Won't Have About Raising Men

September 17, 2014

On Thursday night, the Baltimore Ravens took on the Pittsburgh Steelers. The event carried national significance thanks to the Ravens' public-induced decision to cut running back Ray Rice after tape emerged of Rice clocking his then-fiancee in the head, knocking her out cold. CBS sportscaster James Brown utilized his pregame show to draw attention to the problem of domestic violence -- and suggest widespread culpability for domestic violence. "Our language is important," Brown suggested. "For instance, when a guy says, 'You throw the ball like a girl' or 'You're a little sissy,' it reflects an attitude that devalues women, and attitudes will eventually manifest in some fashion."

Brown wasn't the only commentator to blame "The Sandlot" for Ray Rice's horrifying Mike Tyson-esque blow to his future wife's head. ESPN commentator Kate Fagan explained, "This is behavior that is happening at the grassroots level that is born through years of our culture like raising men to want to not be like women and using language like 'sissy' and 'you throw like a girl' that demean women. ... [We need to focus on] really reprogramming how we raise men."

Naturally, this talking point was celebrated far and wide by a mainstream press more interested in perpetuating the tenets of political correctness than in actually fighting domestic abuse. The real solution to domestic abuse is twofold: punishing it to the greatest possible extent, and yes, raising young men differently. But to state that the greatest risk factor for future domestic violence is insulting other boys as "throwing like girls" is pure idiocy. No man has ever hit a woman because she "throws like a girl." But plenty of young men have hit women because they had no moral compass and did not believe in basic concepts of virtue -- and plenty of young men lack such a moral compass and belief in virtue thanks to lack of male role models.

Teaching respect for women begins with ensuring that solid male influences models fill the lives of young men -- men who respect women, cherish them, treasure them, and believe in protecting them. This is an unpopular stance, because it suggests that boys require men to raise them. Which they do. But that truth doesn't fit the logic of the left, which seems to think that lack of fathers counts less than rhetorically bothersome phrases.

For leftists, the answer to domestic violence isn't to deal with any of the issues that could lead boys to become abusing men. The answer, instead, is to lecture Americans about the use of the word "sissy" -- not because that solves the problem, but because it makes those on the left feel warm and fuzzy inside. Similarly, the left will tell Americans that the name of the Washington Redskins matters far more to Native-Americans than the nearly half of Native-American youths who drop out of high school; they will explain that "microaggressions" are the true problem faced by blacks in America, not lack of education, poverty or unwed motherhood.

We extol the language police even as we castigate moral authorities. And so our problems grow worse. But at least we feel better about them.

A Moral Universe Torn Apart

September 24, 2014

"I am not ashamed," a young woman says into a camera. "I am not ashamed."

The woman is Leyla Josephine of Glasgow, and she is a self-described feminist performance artist. She is reading a poem titled "I Think She Was a She" -- a poem lauded by The Huffington Post as "unapologetic. ... She ardently declares her power over her body as she reminds us that a woman exercising her right to choose is not uncommon -- and should never be shamefully brushed under the rug."

What, exactly, is this poem? It's Josephine recounting her abortion of her unborn daughter. She notes, "I know she was a she and I think she would've looked exactly like me. I would've told her stories about her grandfather, we could've fed the swans at Victoria Park." Then, however, she reveals just what she's done: "I would've supported her right to choose. To choose a life for herself, a path for herself. I would've died for that right like she died for mine. I'm sorry, but you came at the wrong time."

You came at the wrong time. Therefore, murder is justified.

At least Josephine has the intellectual honesty to admit that her daughter was in fact a daughter, not some fictional ball of tissue. But by blithely signing away her daughter's life in the name of convenience, Josephine becomes the emissary of a deep and abiding evil. Her lie that she would lay down her life for the right of her child to choose life, when it is eminently clear that she would not even sacrifice an iota of inconvenience to avoid killing her own child, is morally sickening. Her child did not choose to die for her convenience. Her child had no such choice.

But Josephine doesn't care. "Don't you mutter murder on me," Josephine spits.

Meanwhile, an ocean away, the creator of Obamacare, Dr. Ezekiel Emanuel, has written an equally nausea-inducing piece in which he stumps for death at 75 years of age. Not merely death for himself, mind you -- death for everyone. "My father illustrates the situation well," Emanuel writes, in coldly eugenic fashion. "About a decade ago, just shy of his 77th birthday, he began having pain in his abdomen. ... He had in fact had a heart attack, which led to a cardiac catheterization and ultimately a bypass. Since then, he has not been the same." Emanuel's father is 87, and says he is happy. That doesn't matter. He's no longer useful, according to Emanuel.

Emanuel sees wondrous good for the rest of us in sending the elderly to the "Logan's Run" carousel -- after all, "We want to be remembered as independent, not experienced as burdens ... [leaving our grandchildren] with memories framed not by our vivacity but by our frailty is the ultimate tragedy."

This is the cult of death created by a society that values amusement over life. Amusement means that the death of others is second priority; amusement means that if your own capacity diminishes, your raison d'etre has ended.

If America was built on life, liberty and pursuit of happiness, today's leftist death cult devalues the first and destroys the second in pursuit of the third. And, in the end, there will be no happiness, for happiness is not ceaseless hedonism but living a moral and responsible life. Apparently, we dismissed that definition of happiness long ago. The result: an un-civilization of Leyla Josephines and Ezekiel Emanuels.

The Throat-Clearing President Versus the Throat-Cutting Terrorists

October 1, 2014

Last week, President Obama spoke to the United Nations about the growing threat of the Islamic State in Iraq and Syria. In the course of that speech, he discussed a wide variety of threats to Western civilization, ranging from Ebola to global warming, from chaos in Syria to China's incursions in the South China Sea. The speech seemed unfocused, meandering. But it held together thanks to one common thread: Barack Obama believes that words solve everything. Particularly his own.

Obama's narcissism isn't mere arrogance. It's messianism. It's pure faith that his verbiage can alter the course of history. "We are here," Obama said, "because others realized that we gain more from cooperation than conquest." Well, actually, no -- the United Nations exists because evil nations were forced through conquest to admit that cooperation might be a more advantageous strategy.

"While small gains can be won at the barrel of a gun," Obama said, "they will ultimately be turned back if enough voices support the freedom of nations and peoples to make their own decisions." Not exactly -- millions of voices in North Korea have not altered the fate of those stuck in the world's largest gulag, nor have millions of voices in Iran freed them of the tyranny of the mullahs.

"The ideology of ISIL or al Qaeda or Boko Haram will wilt and die if it is consistently exposed, confronted, and refuted in the light of day," Obama spouted. If good argument killed bad argument, Islamism wouldn't be on the march, but on the ash heap of history. Global politics, it turns out, is not a Harvard Law mock trial.

"We believe that right makes might," Obama summed up, "that bigger nations should not be able to bully smaller ones, that people should be able to choose their own future." Hogwash would be too kind a word to describe this sort of highfaluting idiocy -- if right made might, millions of Jews would still populate Europe.

In reality, right dictates that right arm itself -- right must become might in order to emerge victorious. Americans know that.

Because Americans know that, Obama must occasionally bow to reality. And so, in the same speech in which Obama called for Russian, Chinese and Syrian conflicts to be resolved through diplomacy, he uttered the most un-Obamaesque comment of his entire presidency with regard to ISIS: "The only language understood by killers like this is the language of force."

This is eminently true. It is also so far out of Obama's wheelhouse that he almost strained an oblique in making that statement. And, in fact, when polling doesn't apply to him, Obama is happy to pressure other nations not to use the language of force -- in the same speech, Obama pressured Israel to negotiate with its enemies, even though its enemies are of the exact same ilk as ISIS. If Obama does not bear a striking animus for the Jewish state, the best that can be said is that he wants Israel to be on the cutting edge of Western civilization's rhetoric-first throat-cutting. After all, Obama tells Israel, too many Israelis are "ready to abandon the hard work of peace."

Yes, the hard work of peace. With people who want to slit their throats.

That's the real Obama, not the puffed-chest commander-in-chief threatening to bomb virtually everyone in virtually every country in the Middle East.

And that's the problem. Lack of foreign policy comes from lack of belief in the principled use of force. And so Obama, the messianic narcissist, vacillates between two extremes: empty threats and pathetic wheedling. Neither works.

Rise of the Barbarians

October 8, 2014

On Friday night, a Huntington Beach man, 43, was walking back to his car after the Los Angeles Angels played the Kansas City Royals in the American League Division Series. Three men accosted him, and then proceeded to beat him senseless. He is currently in critical condition at a local hospital after police found him unconscious.

I didn't find the story particularly shocking, given that I took my father and two younger sisters to the Angels-Royals game on Thursday night. Throngs packed the stadium -- the team announced the attendance at 43,321. We had bleacher seats, which sold for $68. The team must have also sold standing room tickets, since behind the bleachers -- lines of fans stood three deep, watching the game.

When my family and I arrived at the game, the ushers had not cleared paths through the standing-room crowd for those who wanted to get to their seats. We gently edged our way toward the seats.

Which is when I heard a guy scream into my ear: "Why the f--- are you bumping me?"

I turned to face a young Hispanic man, wearing a long-sleeved flannel shirt (it was reportedly 93 degrees outside at the time), baggy jeans, an Angels cap cocked off at a bizarre angle, the brim unbent. He wore a close-cropped three-day stubble. He was approximately my height, but probably 20lbs. heavier than I. Two of his friends flanked him.

Though I hadn't bumped, I quickly apologized -- after all, what point is there in a confrontation at a sporting event?

My apology, however, was not accepted. "I said, why the f--- did you bump me?"

Again I apologized. When it became clear that this fellow had downed at least a few beers and had his mind set on some sort of violence, my sister grabbed my arm and we walked away. He glared at me the rest of the game. My sisters focused on reassuring me that getting into a physical fight with the dolt would have served no useful purpose, and could have ended in a 3-on-1 beating. Which didn't make me feel much better.

Unfortunately, this fellow wasn't the only beer-soaked Neanderthal in the bleachers. When a Royals fan, who happened to be black, showed up with his girlfriend, two boozy white Angels fans screamed -- with children in close proximity -- "Go back to f---ing Kansas City!"

It's unlikely any of these charming folks were involved in the beating of the Huntington Beach man after Game 2 of the ALDS. But we now live in a society where young male barbarians are growing in number, their masculinity tied into useless aggression. More and more, young men seem to channel their aggressive instinct not into building, but into destroying -- not into defending the innocent, particularly women and children, but into confrontations for no apparent reason other than demonstrating dominance.

Why?

As a society, we have robbed men of their protective missions. Men who seek to protect women and children are called anti-feminist, gender normative. Men have abandoned their responsibilities to the state. As for building things -- well, there too, men have been told that to build is to act selfishly, without concern for the community. And young men have no male role models, since many of their fathers have abandoned them or abandoned true maleness in pursuit of vainglorious brutality. All of which leads to an increase in destruction by men without purpose, hemmed in only by the power of the state and the benefits of self-interest.

None of this is an excuse for barbarianism, of course. But it does help explain why masculinity used to center around acting like a gentleman, while now it centers around acting like a boor. The more we foster the barbarian mentality, the more barbaric society becomes.

A Bowla Ebola Idiocy

October 15, 2014

On Monday, The Daily Mail reported that NBC's chief medical correspondent, Nancy Snyderman, had a hankering for a bowl of soup from Peasant Grill in Hopewell Boro, New Jersey. So she hopped in her car with one of her crewmembers and headed over to the Grill. When she got to the restaurant, she had her crewmember run inside, grab the soup, and run back out.

There was only one problem: Both Snyderman and her crewmember were under mandatory quarantine for 21 days. That quarantine was a result of their journey to Liberia to cover the Ebola outbreak, a journey during which cameraman Ashoka Mukpo contracted the disease. The authorities made the quarantine mandatory after another of the crewmembers violated a voluntary quarantine last week.

It's one thing for Liberian citizen Thomas Eric Duncan to carry around an Ebola-ridden woman, get on an airplane to Dallas, walk into a hospital with symptoms, and then walk out again. Such behavior can be attributed, at least in part, to ignorance. It's another thing entirely for a highly educated medical professional to endanger those around her for some miso.

But that's the world of the media, where the proper response to the possibility of contracting Ebola is, "Don't you know who I am?" Double standards abound here; media members lather Americans into a frenzy over the threat of a disease that has, to date, claimed a grand total of one life in the United States. Then they go out for lunch in public after being told that they could be carrying the virus.

The Snyderman story is truly part of a broader egocentrism in the media. The media didn't give one whit about the Internal Revenue

Service targeting conservative non-profit applicants -- but they went absolutely batty over the Department of Justice targeting reporters. The media don't seem to care very much about demands for transparency from the Obama administration by the American public -- but they're fighting mad about the Obama administration's refusal to let them photograph him golfing. After all, it's one thing for normal Americans to get stiffed, and quite another for our betters to feel the effects of government's heavy hand.

The gap between the media elite and the general population has a deleterious impact on America's political future. Media members seem to have no problem with incompetent government overreach so long as they prosper, which is why so few media members worry over Democratic proposals to limit First Amendment press freedoms to government-designated "journalists."

The American people suffer thanks to this elitism. The days of the adversarial media are ending -- most investigative journalism now falls to the blogosphere or the foreign press. The corrupt relationship between media and government means that Americans don't find out about overreach and incompetence until far too late for them to do anything about it.

And so the gap grows. No wonder Snyderman went for soup while under quarantine. After all, it's not like all those other customers work for NBC, or anything.

Why Republicans Don't Get It

October 22, 2014

The Republican Party simply doesn't get it.

A new poll this week shows 2012 presidential nominee and 2008 primary candidate Mitt Romney leading the field of potential 2016 Republican candidates. According to ABC News/Washington Post, 21 percent of Republican voters would vote for Romney in the primaries; Jeb Bush and Mike Huckabee tie at 10 percent, followed by Rand Paul, Chris Christie and Paul Ryan. Altogether, some 44 percent of Republican primary voters want an "establishment" candidate -- by which we mean a candidate for whom social issues are secondary, immigration reform is primary and economics dominates.

The establishment donors on the coasts see this poll and believe that a consolidated funding effort mobilized behind the Chosen One (Romney, Bush, Christie or Ryan) could avoid a messy primary and keep the powder dry for a 2016 showdown with Hillary.

The conservative base knows this, and they groan.

That's because the conservative base understands that what motivates them is not the marginal tax rate -- nobody in the country knows, offhand, his or her effective tax rate -- but values. And none of the top priorities for Republican donors match the fire-in-the-belly issues that motivate the folks who knock on doors, phone bank and provide the under-$50 donations that could power a Republican to victory.

The divide between the establishment and the base represents a divide between the wallet and the working man, the penthouse and the pews, the Ivy Leagues and the homeschools. Which is why Republican leadership quietly assures its top donors that should

Republicans win the Senate, their first legislative push will encompass corporate tax reform and immigration reform. They will not push primarily for border security, or for protection of religious freedom, or for repeal of Common Core. They will not use their opportunity to govern as an opportunity to draw contrast between conservatism and leftism. Instead, they will seek "common ground" in a vain attempt to show the American people that efficiency deserves re-election.

And the American people will go to sleep, conservatives will vomit in their mouths, and leftists will demonize Republicans all the same.

Conservatives understand that politics simply reflect underlying values. That's why they are passionate. They don't vote their pocketbooks. They vote their guts, and their guts tell them that leftism is immoral on the most basic level.

Republicans, on the other hand, believe that politics are just business by other means. That means that Republicans think Americans, left and right, share the same underlying values. That's a lie, and it's a self-defeating lie at that.

Until Republicans begin to appreciate the moral conflict between right and left, they will dishearten the right and provide easy targets for the left. The nominee won't matter; elections won't matter. And the alienation of the American conservative will deepen and broaden, until, one day, it bursts forth with a renewed fire that consumes the Republican Party whole.

Turn Down for What?

October 29, 2014

On the way to the airport the other day, my Uber driver, an elderly Russian chap, turned on a Top 40 radio station. Not being one to complain, I actually sat and listened to the lyrics. The song blasting through the speakers of the late-model Honda Civic was titled "Habits." The singer, a young, presumably wealthy Swede named Tove Lo (actual name: Tove Nilsson), warbles about her need to visit sex clubs, do drugs, "binge on all my Twinkies, throw up in the tub." She laments that she "drank up all my money."

Why? Well, she explains, "You're gone and I gotta stay high all the time."

The next song featured a rapper named Lil Jon screaming loudly at the listener that it is "Fire up that loud, another round of shots. ... TURN DOWN FOR WHAT!" Translation: We're drunk and crazed, and we won't stop being drunk and crazed. The music video, as described by creator Daniel Kwan explores, "this other universe where dudes are so pumped up on their own d***s -- and they're so into their testosterone -- that the way that the show that is by breaking s*** with their d***s." The video, which shows a young man crashing through ceilings and into furniture as his erect penis swivels wildly in his pants, currently has nearly 130 million views on YouTube.

No wonder Tove Lo needs to stay high all the time.

The end of Western civilization, it turns out, comes with both a bang and a whimper. The bang: endless sex, animalistic, primal, without strings. As Adam Levine whines, "Baby, I'm preying on you tonight, hunt you down, eat you alive, just like animals, animals, like animals." In 1971, according to the National Survey of Young

Women, 30.4 percent of young women aged 15-19 living in metropolitan areas reported having premarital sex. By 1979, that number was 49.8 percent. Today, 62 percent of young women overall have had premarital sex according to the Centers for Disease Control. In 1950, men's median age of first marriage stood at 22.8; today, it stands at 28.2. More people having sex younger, and without commitment is not a recipe for societal happiness.

Thus the whimper. In a culture in which emotional connections are degraded to the level of bovine rutting, is it any wonder that 9.2 percent of Americans -- some 23.9 million people -- have used an illicit drug in the past month, and that nearly a quarter of those aged 18-20 have done so? Or that nearly a third of men over the age of 12 and 16 percent of women have participated in binge drinking in the last month?

From what are these people running? Drugs and alcohol are an escape -- but we are the most prosperous society on the planet. We are wealthier and healthier than any nation in history. So why the angst?

That question sticks in the craw of the materialists of the secular left, who insist that endless supplies of Soma and government-sponsored sex, complete with Malthusian belt -- to borrow terms from Huxley -- should bring happiness. Obviously, it doesn't. America's suicide rate recently hit a 25-year high. Suicide has surged among the middle-aged, those aged 35-64, jumping 30 percent from 1999 to 2010.

Turn down for what? For survival. Or we could just keep going to sex clubs, throwing up in the bathtub and drinking up all our money. After all, isn't that what freedom from consequences -- our God-given pursuit of happiness, according to the left -- is all about?

Lessons for the GOP for 2016

November 5, 2014

On Tuesday, Republicans won a historic electoral victory, sweeping away a Democratic Senate, replacing Democratic governors in blue states like Massachusetts, Maryland and Illinois, and reversing Democratic state legislatures in Nevada, Colorado, Minnesota, New Mexico, Maine, West Virginia and New Hampshire. Republicans now control more state legislatures than they have at any point since the 1920s, and a bigger House majority than they have since 1928.

The celebratory mood for Republicans pervaded the country -- a feeling of hope, lost since President Obama revealed himself to be just as radical as the right suspected, has returned. That hope isn't vain -- when a landslide of such proportion takes place, there is something to it. The question is whether Republicans can capitalize on their newfound opportunity and finally make a strong move toward winning the White House.

Therein lies the problem. Midterm elections have historically been poor predictors of presidential elections. That's because the crowd that turns out for midterms does not mirror the crowd that turns out for presidential elections -- those who turn out for midterms are more highly motivated and generally better informed. In 2010, for example, approximately 84 million Americans voted for in local Congressional race. In 2012, 108 million Americans voted in the same races. Republicans won about 45 million votes in the Congressional races in 2010, with Democrats coming in far behind at 39 million. In 2012, each party earned about 54 million votes. Of the additional 24 million voters who showed up to vote in Congressional races in 2012, 62.5 percent went for Democrats.

That means that Republicans must not sit on their laurels.

For many in the commentariat, that means that Republicans must push forward a compromising, bipartisan agenda. That seems to be the general opinion of those on the political left, who despise Republicans and who, as the evening of Nov. 4 progressed, strongly resembled Arnold Toht at the end of "Raiders of the Lost Ark," their faces falling with each result.

The truth is precisely the reverse. Republicans cannot be seen as the Party of No, as the GOP's enemies would have it -- but they do have an obligation to turn President Obama into the President of No. That means pushing easily comprehended, single-issue bills, short and clear and popular. If President Obama wants to veto those bills, that becomes his problem. But Republicans should not stop passing legislation between 2014 and 2016.

Meanwhile, Republicans must work to exploit holes in the Democratic base. In 2012, President Obama appealed heavily to minority groups for strong turnout; Hillary Clinton does not have the same minority appeal. That means she will focus strongly on winning single women, and driving them to the polls in large numbers. Republicans should therefore push national security issues, family freedom issues -- and they have just the right faces to do that in Senator Joni Ernst, R-Iowa and Mia Love, R-Utah, among others.

Conservatives can see a ray of sunshine at last. Now they must work to ensure that the ray of sunshine doesn't turn into another faded opportunity.

America's Education Crisis

November 12, 2014

An educational crisis has struck Minneapolis' public schools: Black students have a tenfold higher chance of suspension or expulsion than white students. And superintendent Bernadeia Johnson wants to "disrupt that in any way that I can."

Her solution: refusing to suspend black and Hispanic students. "The only way I can think [to solve the disparity] is to take those suspensions back to the individuals and try and probe and ask questions," Johnson explained. Johnson will work with the Department of Education, which originally brought the disparity to light. Now, Johnson will have to review every potential suspension of a non-white, non-Asian student. "Changing the trajectory for our students of color is a moral and ethical imperative, and our actions must be drastically different to achieve our goal of closing the achievement gap by 2020," Johnson stated.

Black and Hispanic students in Minneapolis represent 60.3 percent of the student body. Just 15 percent of teachers are non-white. This has led to pressure to oust some white teachers in favor of minority teachers. But Minnesota has some of the highest-performing students in the nation: Overall, 70 percent of fourth-graders read at or above grade level, as opposed to 34 percent of students nationally; for eighth-graders, 82 percent of students score above grade level, as opposed to 43 percent nationally. The big problem: Black and Hispanic students score extraordinarily low when compared to white students. Is that because the teachers somehow teach better to white and Asian students? Or is the problem with the students?

The students in Minnesota are not an exception. Male black, Hispanic and Native-American students in every state in America lead male students of other ethnicities in suspensions. That's not due to some inherent disadvantage attached to race, of course. It's because black, Hispanic and Native-American children are disproportionately likely to live with single mothers. And children living with single mothers misbehave more often than those living with fathers. A study from Great Britain of 14,000 children showed that children were twice as likely to manifest behavioral problems by the age of 7 than those raised by their natural parents. Those numbers continue to diverge as children grow older.

But instead of dealing with the obvious problem, the government insists that the problem, somehow, lies in the strictness of the Minneapolis public schools. That's inane. School discipline in Asia far outstrips discipline in the United States. Unsurprisingly, school performance in Asia far outstrips school performance in the United States.

The left in America believes that overlooking actual solutions in favor of happy talk about institutional racism helps minority students. It achieves precisely the opposite, making light of misbehavior and destroying the chances for better education for those who seek to gain it.

The achievement gap will never be closed, so long as school districts across the country punish good students, reward bad ones and let political correctness trump educational necessity.

The Ferguson Days of Rage

November 19, 2014

This week, America held its collective breath as it waited on the grand jury indictment verdict for Officer Darren Wilson. Wilson, you'll recall, had the misfortune to run into 6'5", 289-lb. Michael Brown, an 18-year-old black man who had just finished strong-arm robbing a convenience store. Wilson pulled Brown over as he and his accomplice walked in the middle of the street; all available evidence shows that Brown then pushed himself through the driver's side window, punched Wilson, went for his gun, was shot in the hand, ran, turned around, charged Wilson, and was shot to death.

But that doesn't matter. And it has never mattered. Because facts do not matter to those attempting to rectify what they perceive as an unjust universe. For those utopian visionaries - and, yes, violent thugs who rob stores are minions of the utopian visionaries -- individuals do not exist. Individuals are merely stand-ins for groups. Wilson was a white cop; therefore, he was the Racist White Establishment. Brown was a black teenager; therefore, he was the Innocent Black Victim. The parts have already been written; Wilson was merely unlucky enough to land the starring role.

And so we expect riots no matter what the outcome of the indictment. Should Wilson escape indictment due to complete lack of evidence, the utopians and their rioting henchmen will attribute that acquittal to the Racist White Establishment. Should he be indicted, the utopians and their rioting henchmen will cite Wilson as merely the latest example of the Racist White Establishment. No matter the antecedent, the consequence has been determined in advance: rage, riots, recriminations.

If all of this sounds familiar, that's because it is. Alongside the anti-Racist White Establishment protesters taking to the streets in Ferguson in recent weeks, anti-Israel and pro-ISIS protesters have appeared. All utopian visionaries fighting the status quo -- self-perceived victims -- love their Days of Rage. And these Ragers don't require evidence to incite their emotions. Evidence regarding individuals is for the reasonable; false stories of victims and villains are the fodder for Ragers.

Whether we're watching thousands of Muslims across the world protest and riot over cartoons of Mohammed, or whether we're watching hundreds of people in Ferguson riot over a media-manufactured story about a racial killing, Days of Rage provide the outlet for delusional anger. Radical Muslims need an external enemy to justify their own brutality; protesters in Ferguson need an external enemy to justify their own failure to make good in the freest country in the history of humanity.

Every society has its Ragers. The West's suicidal impulse to humor those Ragers, however, spells the end of the West. When facts become secondary to emotion, truth dies. And a society that doesn't value truth cannot survive. Calling out the National Guard in Ferguson while lending a sympathetic ear to the Ragers does little good, long-term. It merely staves off the inevitable surrender of the reasonable to the Ragers.

Feelingstown, Missouri

November 26, 2014

On Monday night, St. Louis County Prosecuting Attorney Robert McCulloch announced that Officer Darren Wilson, who is white, would not be indicted in the shooting death of black 18-year-old Michael Brown. McCulloch explained the falsehoods permeating the original media accounts of the shooting; he explained that Brown had, by all available physical and credible witness evidence, charged Wilson after attempting to take his gun from him in Wilson's vehicle.

And none of it mattered. The riots went forward as planned; the media steadfastly distributed its prewritten narrative of evil racist white cop murdering innocent young black man. President Obama stepped to the microphones to denounce American racism. He did not recapitulate the evidence; he did not condemn rioters and pledge that law enforcement would crack down on them. Instead, he said that protesters and rioters -- all of them ignoring the fact that a white police officer had not murdered an innocent black man in cold blood -- were justified in their rage.

Indeed, the president said, they had feelings. And those feelings were legitimate, all evidence to the contrary. "There are Americans who agree with it, and there are Americans who are deeply disappointed, even angry. It's an understandable reaction," Obama said. What made disappointment and anger over an evidence-based verdict "understandable"? Obama explained: "There are still problems and communities of color aren't just making these problems up. Separating that from this particular decision, there are issues in which the law too often feels as if it is being applied in a discriminatory fashion."

The key word: feels. Obama did not cite a single instance of the law being applied in a discriminatory fashion -- because in Ferguson it was not. Instead, he made a general statement, of the sort leftists often make, that broad feelings of discontent must be inherently legitimate -- because, after all, if people feel, those feelings must have a basis.

Now, there are certainly individual instances of racism by law enforcement in American society. All such instances should be investigated and prosecuted. But to suggest, as President Obama and the media do, that such instances provide the basis for a justifiable and generalized feeling of discontent is to declare the war on racist activity unwinnable. We cannot fight a shadow-enemy. We can never overcome feelings on a public policy level.

That is why President Obama and the left love discussing feelings. Talking about feelings avoids more difficult conversations about prosecuting individual cases or fighting crime. Feelingstalk means evidence becomes irrelevant because we need no evidence for our feelings -- they are legitimized by virtue of their very being. Self-definition becomes societal definition: if I feel there's a social problem, there's a social problem. In fact, in Feelingstown, facts become insults: If facts debunk feelings, it is the facts that must lose.

Truth is the first casualty of the feelings society; morality is the second.

Civilization is the third. If feelings require no justification in order to receive the presidential seal of approval, we have moved beyond rational political debate. If those feelings require social change, problems become inherently unsolvable.

And so, on to the next Ferguson. Feelings required. No evidence necessary.

The Real Racist Conspiracy In Ferguson

December 3, 2014

After a grand jury in St. Louis, Missouri, voted against the indictment of Officer Darren Wilson in the killing of 18-year-old black man Michael Brown, President Obama gave a short address to the nation. In it, he said he understood why some would feel disappointed at the verdict -- an odd statement, given that all available evidence showed that Brown had robbed a convenience store, attacked Wilson in his vehicle, attempted to grab his gun and charged Wilson before Wilson shot him.

Then Obama dropped a doozy: "We need to recognize that this is not just an issue in Ferguson, this is an issue for America ... there are problems and communities of color aren't just making these problems up."

Obama did not specify what problems he wanted to discuss. Nor did he explain why Ferguson's issues were America's. But the largest lie was the notion that "communities of color" don't make problems up.

Because in Ferguson, that's precisely what a community of color did.

In the immediate aftermath of the Brown shooting, grand jury documents show, witness intimidation and lying became the order of the day. Witness after witness told police that local thugs were intimidating those who had seen the events. One witness told police, according to the St. Louis Police Investigative Report, that threats "had been made to the residents of Canfield Green Apartment Complex." This witness said that "notes had been posted on various apartment buildings threatening people not to talk to the police, and gunshots were still being fired every night."

The witness wasn't alone. Other witnesses stated that supposed witnesses were lying to the media about events, that others who had seen the events were "embellishing their stories" in order to convict Wilson. One witness stated, "You have to understand the mentality of some of these young guys they have nothing to do. When they can latch on the something they embellish it because they want something to do."

Some 16 witnesses testified that Brown's hands were up when he was shot, which was factually false according to the autopsy. Another 12 witnesses said that Wilson shot Brown from behind -- again, false according to the autopsy. One witness testified that Wilson used both a Taser and a gun -- false. Another said that Brown had kneeled before Wilson shot him. When confronted with the fact that the physical evidence made such an account impossible, the witness acknowledged he hadn't seen the event, and then asked if he could leave the grand jury because he was "uncomfortable."

In 1964, Kitty Genovese was stabbed to death outside her apartment complex in New York. The entire nation gasped in horror when it learned that supposed witnesses had not called the police.

Fifty years later, the nation completely ignores the fact that an entire community apparently lied, facilitated lying or intimidated witnesses in order to put an innocent man behind bars, because he happened to be white. At least Kitty Genovese's neighbors didn't actually murder her. Members of the Ferguson community tried to murder Darren Wilson by putting him on death row. Meanwhile, President Obama and those in the media who played up the original narrative cheered them on.

To The Left, Lying About Rape
Is Just Dandy

December 10, 2014

   This week, Rolling Stone printed an editor's note retracting one of the most highly praised pieces of investigative journalism in its history. That piece, written by Sabrina Rubin Erdely, alleged that several members of the University of Virginia fraternity Phi Kappa Psi, had raped a 19-year-old student named Jackie, including with foreign objects, as she lay on a floor covered with broken glass. The article resulted in the university suspending the fraternity's activities, and national outrage over the so-called "rape culture" on campus.

   That rape culture supposedly leads to one in five women being sexually assaulted on campus -- a faulty statistic from a poll that didn't even ask women if they were raped or sexually assaulted, and instead defined sex while inebriated at any level as rape. With regard to reported rape, the federal government reports a rate of just 1.3 per 1,000 Americans. That is, of course, far too high. But it is not a rape culture by any plausible definition.

   Nonetheless, the narrative of women as victims of brutish male society must be forwarded at all costs, for political purposes. If Americans are brutish sexists waiting to rape unsuspecting women, bigger government becomes a necessity. That's why President Obama has cited that one-in-five statistic, and suggested that America experiences "quiet tolerance of sexual assault."

   In order to forward that narrative, all rape stories are treated as fact sans investigation of any kind. And so Jackie's story of gang rape received plaudits across the media landscape.

   Then it fell apart.

The Washington Post quickly debunked the story. According to the Post, the fraternity says there was no event the night Jackie was allegedly raped, Jackie's friends "have not been able to verify key points in recent days," and one of the men named in Jackie's report stated that "he never met Jackie in person and never took her out on a date."

As the Rolling Stone report collapsed, members of the left jumped to defend Jackie. Sally Kohn of CNN.com tweeted that people should stop questioning Jackie's story: "While aspects of UVA rape story now in question, still unsettles me that pouncing by skeptics mirrored sort of doubt rape victims often face." Feminist Melissa McEwan wrote, "If Jackie's story is partially or wholly untrue, it doesn't validate the reasons for disbelieving her."

Under this logic, Atticus Finch was the villain in "To Kill a Mockingbird." After all, how dare he question the rape allegations of a victimized woman and defend Tom Robinson?

But for the left, it's narrative first, facts second.

The same holds true regarding allegations made by HBO star Lena Dunham, who wrote of her own alleged rape at the hands of an Oberlin "college Republican" named Barry. When it turned out that Barry, a readily identifiable person from Dunham's days at Oberlin, did not rape her, the media largely went silent; Dunham still has not spoken on the issue.

Narrative first. Facts second.

Here is the reality: All decent human beings believe that rape is evil. They also believe that false allegations of rape are wrong. These two positions are not mutually exclusive. They complement one another. False rape allegations do actual rape victims a tremendous disservice: to lump in false accusations of rape with true accusations of rape makes people more skeptical of rape victims generally, a horrible result. Rape should be taken seriously; rape accusations should be taken seriously. That means taking factual questions seriously, not merely throwing the word "rape" around casually, without evidence, and without regard for truth.

The Suicidal Hashtags of the West

December 17, 2014

On Monday, Australian police stormed the Lindt Chocolate Cafe in Sydney, where an Islamist terrorist named Man Haron Monis had taken dozens of hostages and held them for 17 hours. Three people were killed, including Monis, and several others were wounded. Monis, an Iranian immigrant, had a long criminal record, including 40 charges for indecent and sexual assault, as well as an outstanding charge for accessory to murder in the killing of his ex-wife. Before his death, Monis requested an ISIS flag, and forced hostages to hold up the so-called Shahada flag, which proclaims in Arabic, "There Is No God But Allah, and Muhammad Is His Messenger."

In response to this Islamist terror attack on a civilian hub in the center of their city, Australians all over the country took action: They tweeted with the hashtag #illridewithyou. This hashtag came from the mind of one Rachel Jacobs, who witnessed a Muslim woman removing her hijab on the local train after the news of the hostage situation broke. Jacobs tweeted, "I ran after her at the train station. I said 'put it back on. I'll walk with u'. She started to cry and hugged me for about a minute -- then walked off alone." Soon, the hashtag had been launched, and quickly trended globally.

Australia's race discrimination commissioner, Tim Soutphommasane, added, "Let's not allow fear, hatred and division to triumph."

Yes, Australia has a race commissioner, but nobody who thinks it's a bad idea to let Islamist fanatics immigrate, or to keep those same Islamist fanatics in jail after they're charged in the stabbing of their ex-wives.

Priorities!

Never mind that nobody had said a word to the woman in the hijab -- pre-emptive anti-Islamophobia was the first response to an Islamist taking Western hostages in a Western capital.

Across the globe, in the United States, two dueling hashtags debated the relative guilt of American law enforcement. After New York City man Eric Garner resisted arrest, and then died thanks to his pre-existing health conditions after being taken down by police, the hashtag #ICantBreathe went viral. That hashtag fought for prominence with one dedicated to Michael Brown, the 18-year-old black man who was shot to death after attempting to take a gun from a police officer and charging the police officer: #HandsUpDontShoot. Never mind that the first hashtag was taken wildly out of context -- Garner was not choked to death -- and that the second was completely fictitious -- autopsy showed Brown did not have his hands up when he was shot.

These hashtags aren't just the work of lazy activists with nothing better to do. They're signifiers of a suicidal west that believes it bears bloodguilt. No real allegations of Islamophobia or racism are necessary -- those can be assumed. We immediately go into preliminary disassociation mode, attempting to demonstrate to our friends and neighbors that while our civilization may be Islamophobic and racist, we are not. After all, we even tweeted using the day's popular hashtag!

Here's the problem: Islamists don't care about hashtags when they can take hostages and earn the sympathetic hashtags of others. Those who resist law enforcement or attack police officers outright are happy to do so when they become causes celebre, no matter what they do wrong.

The West has its evils. There are instances of racism and Islamophobia. Nobody with a brain would deny that. But to slander the West with a sort of communal guilt for an Original Sin, even as the West is under fire from those who would seek to destroy its civilizational foundations, is nothing less than barbaric.

Jeb Bush Vs. Ted Cruz

December 24, 2014

Last week, former Florida Governor Jeb Bush announced his intention to "actively explore" a run for president. That announcement spurred spasms of joy in some segments of the Republican Party who have been itching for an effective counter to the enthusiasm of the grassroots right. Those Republicans -- largely coastal donors who scorn social conservatives as rubes, and shun the supposed fiscal extremism of the tea party -- have been searching for a candidate who will buck the base on immigration, who doesn't mind hand-in-glove corporatism, and who, most of all, feels the same way they do about the grassroots.

And Jeb Bush promises to fulfill all these criteria. He says he feels "a little out of step with my party" on immigration and recently said that illegal immigration wasn't a "felony" but an "act of love"; his support for Common Core has more than a whiff of cronyism to it; just weeks ago, he told The Wall Street Journal that he would be willing to "lose the primary to win the general without violating [his] principles."

This is the dirty secret of the modern Republican Party: For all the talk about grassroots exasperation with the Republican elites, it is the Republican elites who despise the grassroots. Republican elites do not believe in the dismantling of the welfare state; they believe in its maintenance. They do not believe in the unsophisticated free marketeering of the tea party; they believe in a strong government hand on the economic tiller, so long as that hand is benevolent toward their friends. They do not believe in small government; they believe in large government that serves their ends. If given the choice, a few would even select Hillary Clinton as president over Texas Senator Ted Cruz.

They stake their claim to leadership of the Republican Party on the nonsensical notion that they have a record of victory. Pointing to the dramatic implosions of candidates like Delaware's Christine O'Donnell, who primaried Mike Castle only to be blown out by Chris Coons in her Senatorial race, and Sharron Angle, who lost to Senate Majority Leader Harry Reid, establishment Republicans state that they -- and only they -- know how to win elections. They abide by "The Price Is Right" strategy for electoral victory: campaign just to the right of the Democratic candidate in the hopes that you will win everyone to that candidate's right. The magical middle, in this view, is where victory lies.

And so, in 2008, in an election in which Americans resonated to the theme of war weariness, Republicans establishment geniuses touted a Senator most famous for his foreign policy interventionism. In 2012, coming off an election in which Republicans won a stunning victory thanks to popular hatred of Obamacare, Republicans ran the only man in America outside of Barack Obama to implement Obamacare. Grassroots conservatives reluctantly went along with these nominees after failing to unify around an alternative.

Now, in 2016, when Americans have reacted with outrage to President Obama's executive amnesty, and when Hillary Clinton is likely to be the Democratic nominee, establishment Republicans want to run a man whose most famous position is warmth for illegal immigration and is famously chummy with the Clintons (he gave Hillary an award in 2013 for public service).

Why nominate this man? The most common explanation: His widely perceived alternative, grassroots favorite, Ted Cruz, cannot win. Cruz, establishment Republicans say, polarizes instead of unifying; he alienates rather than attracting. But that notion springs, once again, from "The Price Is Right" strategy: If the middle voter is your target, Cruz isn't your man. But the middle voter was Mitt Romney's target in 2012, and he got him -- Romney won independents 50-45, but lost the election by five million votes. The middle voter was John McCain's target, too -- so much so that

McCain considered naming Democratic Senator Joe Lieberman as his running mate. He lost decisively, too.

Will Ted Cruz lose more decisively than either of his predecessors? That's a possibility. But margin of loss is significantly less important than the direction of the political narrative. Party insiders see the 1964 nomination of right-wing Barry Goldwater as a massive defeat. Those outside the party infrastructure see it for what it was: a ground shift in Republican politics that led to the rise of Ronald Reagan. Better to nominate someone who will change the conversation and lose than someone who will reinforce that the parties stand for the same tired politics of failure.

Or, perhaps, Cruz doesn't lose at all. Perhaps it turns out that voters are driven by vision and passion rather than bromides from the Yorks and Lancasters of American politics. Perhaps Ted Cruz, or someone like him, actually animates people rather than treating them like widgets to be manipulated by those born to the purple. Perhaps politics isn't "The Price Is Right."

Return of the 1960s

December 31, 2014

In 2007, then-Senator Barack Obama signified that he represented a sea-change in the nature of American politics. Obama proclaimed that as a member of the younger generation -- born in 1961, at the tail end of the baby boom -- he no longer wanted to participate in the stale and tired politics of the 1960s. Instead, he wanted to thrust America forward into a "different kind of politics," one beyond the "psychodrama of the baby-boom generation -- a tale rooted in old grudges and revenge plots hatched on a handful of college campuses long ago -- played out on the national stage."

Like most of what President Obama said, this turned out to be a lie. President Obama isn't merely a reflection of 1960s politics. He represents a return to those ugly politics: the nastiness of anti-cop sentiment, the divisiveness of generalized anti-Western foreign policy, the idiocy of a war between the sexes and against the exclusivity of the traditional family structure. President Obama isn't representative of a new breed. He is the child of the 1960s politics he once claimed to abhor.

Those politics, at least, had the excuse of an uglier America -- one fresh with the wounds of Jim Crow, the sins of sexism, the controversy of Vietnam. Today's 1960s reruns seem wildly out of context. But that's the point: For the radicals of the 1960s, just as for the establishment Obamaites of today, context simply does not matter. When you are attempting to craft utopia, context is irrelevant -- and human beings become either tools or obstacles toward the creation of that utopia. The vision never changes. Only the calendar does.

And so we're watching racial tensions on a scale unseen since the 1970s play out across America -- with the support of the political establishment. The images of police officers turning their backs on New York Mayor Bill De Blasio mirror the images of officers booing New York Mayor John Lindsay in 1972 at the funeral of Officer Rocco Laurie. The images of rioters burning down Ferguson mirror the images of rioters burning down Detroit in 1967. Never mind that America of 2014 is not the America of 1967 or 1972 -- if Obama and his allies have to recreate that chaotic era to forward their own political ends, they will.

We're watching the foreign policy of the hard-left McGovernites re-establish itself, this time from the Oval Office. The images of Senator Dianne Feinstein, D-Calif., railing against the CIA on the floor of the Senate over the CIA's use of enhanced interrogation techniques mirror the images of Senator Mark Hatfield, R-Ore., railing against the American military in the aftermath of the Winter Soldier hearings of 1971. The images of the Yazidis starving on mountaintops in Iraq mirror the images of Vietnamese rushing onto boats to escape the horrors of the communists in the aftermath of the Vietnam War.

We're watching the divisive domestic politics of the social radicals reassert themselves. The images of failed Texas gubernatorial candidate Wendy Davis standing in pink sneakers to list the glories of late-term abortion mirror the images of Gloria Steinem blathering about "reproductive freedom" in 1971. The images of Nancy Pelosi touting freedom from "job lock" thanks to Obamacare mirror the images of President Johnson effectively doing the same thanks to the war on poverty.

President Obama and his ilk quest for a return to hopier, changier times -- times like the 1960s. And so they will take us all back to the future. Sadly, our future will then be no more than a reversion to insanity of our past.

About the Author

Ben Shapiro was born in 1984. He entered the University of California Los Angeles at the age of 16 and graduated summa cum laude and Phi Beta Kappa in June 2004 with a Bachelor of Arts degree in Political Science. He graduated Harvard Law School cum laude in June 2007.

Shapiro was hired by Creators Syndicate at age 17 to become the youngest nationally syndicated columnist in the United States. His columns are printed in major newspapers and websites including *The Riverside Press-Enterprise* and the *Conservative Chronicle*, Townhall.com, ABCNews.com, WorldNetDaily.com, Human Events, FrontPageMag.com, FamilySecurityMatters.com. His columns have appeared in *The Christian Science Monitor, Chicago Sun-Times, Orlando Sentinel, The Honolulu Advertiser, The Arizona Republic, Claremont Review of Books* and RealClearPolitics.com. He has been the subject of articles by *The Wall Street Journal, The New York Times*, The Associated Press, and *The Christian Science Monitor*; he has been quoted on "The Rush Limbaugh Show," "The Dr. Laura Show," at CBSNews.com, in the *New York Press, The Washington Times*, and *The American Conservative*.

The author of the national best-sellers, "Brainwashed: How Universities Indoctrinate America's Youth," "Porn Generation: How Social Liberalism Is Corrupting Our Future," and "Project President: Bad Hair and Botox on the Road to the White House." Shapiro has appeared on hundreds of television and radio shows around the nation, including "The O'Reilly Factor," "Fox and Friends," "In the Money," "DaySide with Linda Vester," "Scarborough Country," "The Dennis Miller Show," "Fox News Live," "Glenn Beck Show," "Your World with Neil Cavuto," "700 Club," "The Laura Ingraham

Show," "The Michael Medved Show," "The G. Gordon Liddy Show," "The Rusty Humphries Show," "The Lars Larson Show," "The Larry Elder Show," The Hugh Hewitt Show" and "The Dennis Prager Show."

Shapiro is married and runs Benjamin Shapiro Legal Consulting in Los Angeles.

A MORAL UNIVERSE TORN APART
is also available as an e-book
for Kindle, Amazon Fire, iPad, Nook and
Android e-readers. Visit
creatorspublishing.com to learn more.

o o o

CREATORS PUBLISHING

We publish books.
We find compelling storytellers and
help them craft their narrative,
distributing their novels and collections
worldwide.

o o o

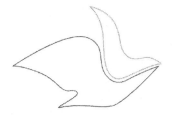

52440270R00078

Made in the USA
San Bernardino, CA
07 September 2019